Linux Command Line Guide

Your Step-by-Step Introduction to
Shell Essentials

Joshua Vicarth

Table of Contents

Chapter 1: Entering the Linux World

Forget fancy windows and icons for a moment; we're going back to the roots of computing interaction, where simple text commands unlock immense power. This chapter is your first step, easing you into what Linux is, why the command line is so useful, and how to start interacting with it.

What is Linux, Really?

You've probably heard the name "Linux" tossed around. Maybe you know it runs servers, or perhaps you've heard of distributions like Ubuntu or Fedora. But what *is* it fundamentally?

A Brief History: From UNIX to Today

Our story begins not with Linux, but with its ancestor: **UNIX**. Developed way back in the late 1960s and early 1970s at Bell Labs, UNIX was a groundbreaking operating system. It introduced many concepts we still use today, like a hierarchical filesystem and the idea of small, specialized command-line tools working together. It was powerful, elegant, and designed by programmers for programmers.

Fast forward to 1991. A Finnish student named Linus Torvalds was tinkering with building his own operating system kernel, partly inspired by UNIX (specifically, a system called Minix) but intended as a free and open alternative. He famously announced his hobby project, noting it wouldn't be "big and professional". Little did he know!

Understanding the Kernel and Distributions

What Linus created was the **Linux kernel**. Think of the kernel as the absolute core of the operating system. It's the engine of the car. It manages the computer's hardware

(CPU, memory, disks), runs programs, and handles all the low-level, essential tasks. But an engine alone isn't a car you can drive easily. You need a chassis, seats, a steering wheel, mirrors, and so on.

That's where **Linux distributions** (or "distros") come in. A distribution takes the Linux kernel and bundles it with other essential software: system utilities (like the tools we'll learn), graphical desktops (like GNOME or KDE), application software (web browsers, office suites), and crucially for us, a **shell** (the command-line interpreter we'll meet shortly). Popular distributions include Ubuntu, Debian, Fedora, CentOS, Arch Linux, and many more. They all use the Linux kernel, but they differ in their included software, package management systems (how you install software, covered in Chapter 13), default settings, and target audience. It's like different car manufacturers using the same type of engine but building very different vehicles around it.

Why Linux? Open Source, Stability, Flexibility

So why has Linux become so popular, especially in servers, supercomputers, and embedded devices (like your Android phone!)?

1. **Open Source:** The source code for the Linux kernel (and most software bundled in distributions) is freely available. Anyone can view, modify, and distribute it. This fosters collaboration, rapid bug fixing, and innovation. It's built by a global community.
2. **Stability:** Linux is renowned for its stability and reliability. Systems can often run for years without needing a reboot. This is crucial for servers that need to be available 24/7.
3. **Flexibility:** Because it's open source and modular, Linux can be adapted for almost any computing task, from tiny sensors to massive server farms, from desktops to smartphones. The command line, in particular, offers unparalleled flexibility in controlling the system.

Meet the Command Line Interface (CLI)

Most people interact with computers using a **Graphical User Interface (GUI)**. Think windows, icons, menus, and pointers (your mouse cursor). You click on things to make them happen. It's visual and often intuitive for common tasks.

The **Command Line Interface (CLI)** is different. It's a text-based way to interact with the computer. You type commands, press Enter, and the computer responds with text output. It might look plain, even archaic, compared to a modern GUI.

Graphical vs. Text-Based Interfaces

Imagine you want to tell your car what to do. The GUI approach is like using the steering wheel, pedals, and dashboard controls – visual and designed for typical driving. The CLI approach is like opening the hood and talking directly to the engine components using a specific technical language. It requires more knowledge, but you can perform fine-tuning and complex operations that aren't possible from the driver's seat alone.

Why Bother with the Terminal? Power and Efficiency

If GUIs are so user-friendly, why learn the CLI?

- **Power:** Many advanced system administration tasks and configurations are *only* available or much easier to perform via the command line.
- **Efficiency:** Once you learn the commands, you can often perform complex tasks much faster by typing a single line than by clicking through multiple windows and menus.
- **Automation:** The CLI is built for scripting. You can easily combine commands to automate repetitive tasks, saving incredible amounts of time. We'll touch on this in Chapter 15.
- **Remote Access:** The standard way to manage remote Linux servers is via the CLI (usually using SSH, which we'll mention below). GUIs are often impractical or unavailable on servers.
- **Resource Usage:** CLIs generally use fewer system resources (memory, CPU) than GUIs.

The Shell: Your Command Interpreter

When you open a terminal window, you're not talking directly to the Linux kernel. You're interacting with a program called the **shell**. The shell acts as an intermediary:

1. It displays a **prompt**, waiting for your input.
2. It reads the command you type.
3. It interprets the command, figures out what program to run, and tells the kernel to execute it.
4. It displays the output of that program back to you in the terminal.

Think of the shell as your translator, speaking the technical language the kernel understands based on the commands you provide. There are several different shells available (like zsh, fish, csh), but the most common and the one we'll focus on is

Bash (Bourne Again SHell). Bash is the default shell on most Linux distributions and macOS.

Getting Access to a Terminal

Okay, enough theory! How do you actually get to this command line? You need a **terminal emulator**. This is a graphical program that gives you access to the shell. Here are the common ways:

- **On a Linux Desktop:** If you're running a Linux distribution with a graphical desktop (like Ubuntu, Fedora, Mint), look for an application called "Terminal", "Konsole", "GNOME Terminal", "XTerm", or something similar in your application menu. Launching it will open a window with a shell prompt, ready for your commands.
- **Connecting Remotely (SSH):** If the Linux system you want to control is on a different machine (like a server in a data center or even another computer on your local network), you'll typically use the **Secure Shell (SSH)** protocol. Programs like `ssh` (on Linux/macOS) or PuTTY (on Windows) allow you to establish a secure connection and get a shell prompt on the remote machine. We'll explore SSH in more detail in Chapter 14.
- **Windows Subsystem for Linux (WSL):** If you're using a modern Windows system, Microsoft provides WSL, which allows you to run a genuine Linux environment (including a shell like Bash) directly on Windows without needing a separate virtual machine. It's a fantastic way to get started. You can install distributions like Ubuntu directly from the Microsoft Store.
- **Virtual Machines (VMs):** You can install software like VirtualBox or VMware, create a virtual machine, and install a full Linux distribution inside it. This keeps it completely separate from your main operating system.
- **Cloud Servers:** Services like AWS, Google Cloud, and Azure let you rent virtual Linux servers in the cloud. You typically connect to these using SSH.

Choose the method that works best for you. For learning, running Linux natively, using WSL, or using a VM are all excellent options.

Your First Commands

Let's type something! Open your terminal. You should see a prompt, which often ends with a $ symbol (or a # if you're logged in as the special 'root' user – avoid that for now!). The text before the symbol usually gives you information like your username and the machine's name.

Type the following command and press Enter:

```
date
```

The system should respond by printing the current date and time:

```
Tue Jul 23 15:30:45 BST 2024
```

Congratulations! You've executed your first command. Let's try another:

```
cal
```

This command displays a simple calendar for the current month:

```
     July 2024
Su Mo Tu We Th Fr Sa
    1  2  3  4  5  6
 7  8  9 10 11 12 13
14 15 16 17 18 19 20
21 22 23 24 25 26 27
28 29 30 31
```

One more – find out who the system thinks you are:

```
whoami
```

It will simply print your username:

```
your_username
```

Understanding Command Structure

These commands look simple, but most commands follow a standard structure:

```
command [options] [arguments]
```

- **Command:** The name of the program you want to run (e.g., date, cal, ls). This part is **mandatory**. Commands are almost always **case-sensitive**; date is not the same as Date or DATE.
- **Options:** These modify the command's behavior. They usually start with one or two dashes (- or --) and are often single letters (like -l) or descriptive

words (like `--human-readable`). Options are **optional**. You can often combine single-letter options (e.g., `-l -a` can often be written as `-la`).

- **Arguments:** These specify *what* the command should operate on, often files or directories (e.g., a filename, a directory path). Arguments are **optional** for many commands, but required for others.

Let's look at an example using the `ls` command (which lists directory contents, covered in Chapter 2), even though we haven't formally introduced it yet. Don't worry about what it does for now, just look at the structure:

```
ls -l /home
```

- `ls`: The command (list directory contents).
- `-l`: An option (use a long listing format).
- `/home`: An argument (the specific directory to list).

We'll dissect `ls` thoroughly in the next chapter. For now, remember the `command [options] [arguments]` pattern and the importance of **case sensitivity**.

Exiting the Shell

When you're finished with your terminal session, you can close it in a couple of ways:

1. Type the `exit` command and press Enter.
2. Press the key combination `Ctrl+d`.

Either of these will terminate the shell process and likely close the terminal window or disconnect your SSH session.

Chapter Summary

We've taken our first steps into the powerful realm of the Linux command line. You've learned that Linux is a kernel, usually bundled into distributions, and valued for its open-source nature, stability, and flexibility. We contrasted the text-based Command Line Interface (CLI) with graphical interfaces, highlighting the CLI's advantages in power, efficiency, and automation. You now know that you interact with the system via a shell (like Bash) running in a terminal emulator. We even ran our first few commands (`date`, `cal`, `whoami`), learned the basic command structure (`command [options] [arguments]`), and saw how to exit the shell.

You might feel like you're just scratching the surface, and you are! But you've built a foundation. In the next chapter, we'll learn how to navigate the Linux filesystem – finding out where you are, listing files, and moving between directories. Let's keep exploring!

Chapter 2: Finding Your Way Around

Welcome back! In Chapter 1, we dipped our toes into the Linux world, met the command line, and ran a few basic commands. Now, it's time to learn how to navigate. Imagine being dropped into a new city without a map – you'd want to know how to figure out where you are and how to get to different places, right? This chapter is your map to the Linux **filesystem**. We'll explore its structure and learn the essential commands for moving around and viewing its contents: `pwd`, `ls`, and `cd`. Let's start exploring your system's layout.

The Linux Filesystem Structure

Unlike operating systems like Windows which might have separate drives (C:, D:), the Linux filesystem is one big, unified tree structure. Everything starts from a single top-level directory called the **root directory**, represented by a forward slash (/).

Everything is a File (Almost!)

A core philosophy in UNIX and Linux is the idea that *everything is treated like a file*. This includes not just the documents and programs you'd expect, but also directories, hardware devices (like your hard drive, keyboard, or printer), and even certain system information interfaces. This might seem strange at first, but it provides a consistent way for commands to interact with different system resources. For now, just keep this idea in the back of your mind; its elegance becomes more apparent as you learn more.

Key Directories

Starting from the root directory (/), several standard directories hold specific types of files. While the exact contents can vary slightly between distributions, understanding these key locations is crucial:

- /: The **root directory**. Everything on the system resides under this directory.
- /home: Contains personal directories for each regular user on the system. If your username is ada, your personal files will likely be in /home/ada. This is where you'll usually store your documents, downloads, pictures, etc.
- /bin: Holds essential **binary** executables (programs) needed for the system to function, even in single-user mode. Many basic commands like ls, cp, mv live here.
- /sbin: Contains essential **system binaries**, typically commands used for system administration tasks that only the superuser (root) might need.
- /etc: Stores system-wide **configuration files**. Think settings for the operating system itself and many installed programs. You'll often look here (but rarely edit directly as a beginner) to see how things are configured. The name likely comes from "et cetera," but think "editable text configurations."
- /var: Holds **variable** data files. This includes things that change frequently, like system logs (/var/log), mail spools, printer spools, and temporary files that need to persist across reboots.
- /tmp: A place for **temporary** files. Programs often use this directory to store data they only need briefly. Files here might be deleted automatically when the system reboots.
- /usr: Contains user-installed software, libraries, and documentation. A large portion of your system's applications reside under /usr/bin, libraries under /usr/lib, and documentation under /usr/share/doc. It historically stood for "User System Resources."
- /dev: Contains **device files**. Remember "everything is a file"? This is where Linux represents hardware devices like hard drives (/dev/sda, /dev/nvme0n1), terminals (/dev/tty1), and even null (/dev/null – a black hole for data).

There are other important directories, but these provide a good starting point.

Visualizing the Tree

Imagine an upside-down tree. The / directory is the base of the trunk. Branches like /home, /bin, and /etc sprout from the trunk. Each of these can have further sub-branches (subdirectories). For instance, /home contains branches for each user (/home/ada, /home/charles), and /home/ada might contain further branches like Documents, Pictures, and Downloads.

```
/   (root)
|
+-- bin/
```

```
+-- etc/
+-- home/
|   +-- ada/
|   |   +-- Documents/
|   |   +-- Pictures/
|   +-- charles/
+-- tmp/
+-- usr/
|   +-- bin/
|   +-- lib/
+-- var/
    +-- log/
```

This hierarchical structure allows for organized storage and easy navigation – once you know the commands!

Knowing Where You Are: pwd

When navigating a complex filesystem, it's easy to lose track of your current location. The pwd command is here to help. It stands for "print working directory," and it does exactly that: it tells you the full path of the directory you are currently in.

Type pwd and press Enter:

```
pwd
```

The output will be the **absolute path** to your current directory, starting from the root (/). If you just opened a terminal as user ada, the output might be:

```
/home/ada
```

If you were in the system log directory, it might be:

```
/var/log
```

pwd is a simple but essential command to orient yourself anytime you feel lost in the directory tree.

Listing Files and Directories: ls

Knowing where you are is good, but you also need to see *what's* there. The `ls` command (short for **list**) is used to list the contents of a directory.

Basic Listing

If you run `ls` without any options or arguments, it lists the contents of the current working directory (pwd):

```
ls
```

The output will show the names of files and subdirectories within your current location, often sorted alphabetically and sometimes color-coded by file type:

```
Desktop  Documents  Downloads  Music  Pictures  Public  Templates  Videos
```

You can also specify a directory to list:

```
ls /bin
```

This will show you a list (potentially very long!) of the essential command binaries stored in the /bin directory.

Seeing Details: -l (Long Listing)

The basic `ls` output only shows names. To get more information, use the -l option for a **long listing format**:

```
ls -l
```

This provides a much more detailed view, with each file or directory on its own line:

```
total 48
drwxr-xr-x 2 ada   users 4096 Jul 20 10:00 Desktop
drwxr-xr-x 5 ada   users 4096 Jul 23 09:15 Documents
drwxr-xr-x 2 ada   users 4096 Jul 23 14:55 Downloads
-rw-r--r-- 1 ada   users  896 Jul 15 11:30 my_notes.txt
drwxr-xr-x 2 ada   users 4096 Jun 10 16:22 Music
drwxr-xr-x 3 ada   users 4096 Jun 12 08:40 Pictures
-rwxr-xr-x 1 ada   users 9128 Jul 21 17:01 process_data.sh
```

```
drwxr-xr-x 2 root root  4096 May 01 13:00 shared_folder
```

There's a lot of information here! Let's break down that first column (`drwxr-xr-x` or `-rw-r--r--` etc.).

Understanding `ls -l` Output

The `ls -l` output provides several columns of information for each item listed.

Column	Example	Meaning
Type	d or -	File type (d=directory, -=regular file, l=symlink...)
Perms	rwxr-xr-x	Permissions (Read, Write, Execute for User, Group, Others)
Links	2 or 1	Number of hard links to the file
Owner	ada or root	The user who owns the file
Group	users or root	The group that owns the file
Size	4096 or 896	Size of the file in bytes (directories usually show block size)
Date/Time	Jul 23 09:15	Last modification date and time
Name	Documents	The name of the file or directory

We'll delve deep into **Permissions** (like `rwxr-xr-x`) in Chapter 7, as they are fundamental to how Linux controls access to files. For now, recognize that this column tells you who can read, write, or execute a file. The first character tells you the file type (d for directory, - for a regular file).

Showing Hidden Files: `-a`

By default, `ls` hides files and directories whose names begin with a dot (`.`). These are often configuration files or directories used to store application settings (e.g., `.bashrc`, `.config`, `.local`). To see *all* files, including hidden ones, use the `-a` option:

```
ls -a
```

You'll now see entries like `.` and `..` (which we'll discuss next) along with any hidden files or directories:

```
.             .bash_logout  .config    Downloads        Music       .profile   Videos
..            .bashrc       Desktop    .local           my_notes.txt Pictures   Public
.bash_history               Documents  process_data.sh  Templates
```

Combining Options

You can combine multiple single-letter options after a single dash. To get a long listing (-l) of all files (-a), you can use:

```
ls -la
# Or equivalently:
ls -al
```

This is very common practice. Another useful option is -h (human-readable), often used with -l, which displays file sizes in a friendlier format (e.g., 4.0K, 8.8K instead of 4096, 9128):

```
ls -lah

total 48K
drwxr-xr-x 7 ada   users 4.0K Jul 23 15:10 .
drwxr-xr-x 3 root  root  4.0K Jul 19 08:00 ..
-rw------- 1 ada   users 1.2K Jul 23 15:05 .bash_history
# ... other files ...
-rw-r--r-- 1 ada   users  896 Jul 15 11:30 my_notes.txt
drwxr-xr-x 3 ada   users 4.0K Jun 12 08:40 Pictures
-rwxr-xr-x 1 ada   users 8.9K Jul 21 17:01 process_data.sh
drwxr-xr-x 2 root  root  4.0K May 01 13:00 shared_folder
# ... etc ...
```

Experiment with ls and its options! It's one of the commands you'll use most frequently.

Changing Directories: cd

Now that you can see where you are (pwd) and what's around you (ls), how do you move? The cd command (**change directory**) is your vehicle.

Absolute vs. Relative Paths

To tell cd where to go, you provide a **path** as an argument. Paths specify a location in the filesystem tree and come in two flavors:

1. **Absolute Paths:** An absolute path specifies the location starting from the very root (/) of the filesystem. It's like giving a full street address, including the city and country. Examples: /home/ada/Documents, /etc, /var/log. Absolute paths **always start with a** /. They work regardless of your current location.

2. **Relative Paths:** A relative path specifies the location *relative* to your current working directory (pwd). It's like giving directions based on where you are right now ("go down the hall and take the first left"). Examples: `Documents`, `Pictures/Vacation`, `../shared_folder`. Relative paths **do not start with a** /.

Let's say your `pwd` is `/home/ada`.

- To move to the `Documents` directory *within* `/home/ada`, you can use the relative path: `cd Documents`
- To move to the system log directory, you *must* use the absolute path: `cd /var/log`
- If you are in `/home/ada/Documents` and want to go to `/home/ada/Downloads`, you could use the absolute path `cd /home/ada/Downloads` or a relative path (which we'll see how to construct next).

Choosing between absolute and relative paths depends on the situation. Absolute paths are unambiguous but can be longer to type. Relative paths are often shorter for nearby locations but depend on your current directory.

Special Directories: ., .., ~

There are a few special directory notations that are incredibly helpful for relative navigation:

- `.` (A single dot): Represents the **current directory** itself. While `cd .` doesn't move you, `.` is useful in other commands when you need to explicitly refer to the current location.
- `..` (Two dots): Represents the **parent directory** (the directory one level *up* from the current one). This is your way to climb back up the tree.
- `~` (Tilde): Represents your **home directory**. Typing `cd ~` will always take you back to your personal home directory (e.g., `/home/ada`) regardless of where you are currently. Running `cd` with *no arguments* also typically takes you to your home directory.

Navigating Effectively

Let's put `cd` and these special directories into practice. Assume you start in `/home/ada`:

```
pwd
# Output: /home/ada

# Move into Documents using a relative path
cd Documents
```

```
pwd
# Output: /home/ada/Documents

# Move back up to the parent directory (/home/ada)
cd ..
pwd
# Output: /home/ada

# Move into Downloads using a relative path
cd Downloads
pwd
# Output: /home/ada/Downloads

# Move directly to the system config directory using an absolute path
cd /etc
pwd
# Output: /etc

# Go straight back to your home directory
cd ~
pwd
# Output: /home/ada

# Or just:
cd /var/log
pwd
# Output: /var/log
cd
pwd
# Output: /home/ada
```

You can also combine .. to move up multiple levels. If you are in /home/ada/Documents/Reports, cd ../.. would take you up two levels to /home/ada.

Getting comfortable with cd, absolute paths, relative paths, .., and ~ is fundamental to working efficiently on the command line.

Tab Completion: Your Best Friend

Typing long directory or file names is tedious and prone to errors (remember, Linux is case-sensitive!). Luckily, the Bash shell provides a fantastic feature called **tab completion**.

Here's how it works:

1. **Command Completion:** Start typing a command (like `pw`) and press the `Tab` key. If there's only one command starting with `pw`, the shell will automatically complete it to `pwd`. If there are multiple possibilities (e.g., you type `c` and press `Tab`), pressing `Tab` a second time will often list all commands starting with `c`.
2. **Path/Filename Completion:** This is where it shines for navigation. Type `cd Docu` and press `Tab`. If `Documents` is the only file or directory in the current location starting with `Docu`, the shell will complete it to `cd Documents`. If there were others (like `Documentation`), it would complete as far as possible (`cd Docu`) and wait for more input or list the possibilities if you press `Tab` again.

Use tab completion constantly!

- It saves you typing.
- It drastically reduces typos.
- It helps you explore by showing possible completions if you press Tab twice.

Once you get used to hitting `Tab` after typing the first few characters of a command or path, you'll wonder how you ever lived without it.

Chapter Summary

In this chapter, we explored the layout of the Linux filesystem, understanding its hierarchical tree structure rooted at / and the purpose of key directories like /home, /bin, /etc, and /var. You learned how to always know your current location using pwd (print working directory). We spent significant time with the ls (list) command, seeing how to view directory contents, get detailed information with -l, view hidden files with -a, and combine options like -lah for a comprehensive, readable view. Crucially, you learned how to navigate this structure using cd (change directory), mastering the difference between **absolute** and **relative paths** and utilizing the special . (current), .. (parent), and ~ (home) directories. Finally, we introduced the indispensable **tab completion** feature to accelerate your command-line interactions and minimize errors.

You now have the fundamental tools to move around and see what's inside your Linux system. In the next chapter, we'll build on this by learning how to create, copy, move, rename, and delete files and directories – essential skills for managing your work.

Chapter 3: Managing Files and Directories

Alright, you've learned how to navigate the Linux filesystem like a seasoned explorer using `pwd`, `ls`, and `cd`. You know how to find your way around and see what's in each location. That's fantastic! But exploring is only part of the journey. Now, it's time to become an architect – to create, organize, rearrange, and clean up your digital space. In this chapter, we'll roll up our sleeves and learn the essential commands for managing files and directories: `mkdir` for making directories, `touch` for creating empty files, `cp` for copying, `mv` for moving and renaming, and the powerful (and slightly dangerous) `rm` for removing things. Let's start building!

Creating Directories: `mkdir`

Just like organizing physical items into boxes or folders, you'll want to create directories (folders) in Linux to keep your files organized. The command for this is `mkdir` (**make dir**ectory).

Its basic usage is straightforward: you provide the name of the directory you want to create as an argument.

```
# Let's make a directory for some practice files
mkdir practice_files

# Let's verify it was created
ls
```

You should see `practice_files` listed among any other files or directories in your current location.

```
Desktop  Documents  Downloads  Music  Pictures  practice_files  Public ...
```

You can also create multiple directories at once by listing them:

```
mkdir backups scripts logs
ls

backups Desktop Documents Downloads logs Music Pictures practice_files
Public ...
```

Now, what if you want to create a directory structure, like `project/data/raw`? If you try `mkdir project/data/raw` and the `project` or `project/data` directories don't already exist, `mkdir` will give you an error.

```
mkdir project/data/raw

mkdir: cannot create directory 'project/data/raw': No such file or directory
```

This is where the incredibly useful -p option comes in. It stands for **parents**, and it tells `mkdir` to create any necessary parent directories along the way.

```
mkdir -p project/data/raw

# Let's check inside 'project' now
ls project

data

# And inside 'project/data'
ls project/data

raw
```

See? `mkdir -p` created `project`, then `data` inside it, and finally `raw` inside `data`. It's a real time-saver when setting up nested structures.

Creating Empty Files: touch

Sometimes you just need an empty file, perhaps as a placeholder, a log file before anything is written to it, or simply to test something. The `touch` command is perfect for this.

```
# Go into our practice directory
```

```
cd practice_files

# Create an empty file
touch my_first_file.txt

# Verify
ls -l

total 0
-rw-r--r-- 1 your_user your_group 0 Jul 23 16:10 my_first_file.txt
```

Notice the size is 0 bytes. touch simply creates the file metadata if the file doesn't exist. You can also create multiple empty files at once:

```
touch report.log data.csv notes_for_meeting
ls

data.csv  my_first_file.txt  notes_for_meeting  report.log
```

Interestingly, the primary historical purpose of touch isn't actually *creating* files, but rather *updating the timestamps* of existing files. Every file in Linux has timestamps tracking when it was last accessed, modified, or had its metadata changed. If you run touch on a file that already exists, it updates these timestamps to the current time without changing the file's content.

```
# Wait a minute or two...
touch my_first_file.txt

# Check the timestamp again (it will be updated)
ls -l my_first_file.txt

-rw-r--r-- 1 your_user your_group 0 Jul 23 16:12 my_first_file.txt
```

While timestamp manipulation is useful in scripting and development, for beginners, touch is mostly known as the quick way to create an empty file.

Copying Files and Directories: cp

Now that we can create things, let's look at duplicating them. The cp (**copy**) command is your photocopier for the command line.

Copying Files

The basic structure is `cp source destination`.

```
# Create a file with some text (we'll see 'echo' and '>' later)
echo "This is the original file." > original.txt

# Copy it to a new file name
cp original.txt copy_of_original.txt

# Check that both exist
ls


copy_of_original.txt  data.csv  my_first_file.txt notes_for_meeting original.txt
report.log
```

You can also copy a file into a different directory. Let's create a subdirectory first:

```
mkdir backups
cp original.txt backups/

# Check inside the backups directory
ls backups/


original.txt
```

If the destination is a directory, the file is copied *into* that directory with its original name. You can also copy *and* rename at the same time if the destination includes a new filename:

```
cp original.txt backups/original_backup_$(date +%F).txt
ls backups/


original.txt  original_backup_2024-07-23.txt
```

(We used `$(date +%F)` *here to add the current date - a little preview of command substitution from Chapter 15!)*

You can copy multiple files into a directory by listing all the source files before the destination directory:

```
cp report.log data.csv notes_for_meeting backups/
ls backups/
```

```
data.csv notes_for_meeting original.txt original_backup_2024-07-23.txt
report.log
```

Important: If the destination file already exists, cp will usually **overwrite it without warning**! To be prompted before overwriting, use the -i (interactive) option:

```
# Try copying again, prompting before overwrite
cp -i original.txt copy_of_original.txt

cp: overwrite 'copy_of_original.txt'?
```

Type y and Enter to confirm, or n and Enter to cancel that specific copy.

Another helpful option is -v (verbose), which tells cp to show you what it's doing:

```
cp -v original.txt yet_another_copy.txt

'original.txt' -> 'yet_another_copy.txt'
```

Copying Directories

What if you want to copy an entire directory, including all the files and subdirectories inside it? If you try cp backups/ backups_copy, you'll likely get an error because cp by default doesn't copy directories.

```
cp backups backups_copy

cp: -r not specified; omitting directory 'backups'
```

The error message gives you the hint: you need the -r or -R option, which stands for **recursive**. This tells cp to dive into the source directory and copy everything within it.

```
cp -r backups/ backups_copy

# Verify the new directory exists and has content
ls backups_copy/

data.csv notes_for_meeting original.txt original_backup_2024-07-23.txt
report.log
```

You can combine -r with -i and -v (e.g., `cp -riv source_dir dest_dir`) for safer and more informative directory copying.

Moving and Renaming: mv

While `cp` creates duplicates, `mv` (**move**) is used to either physically move files/directories to a different location or simply rename them in their current location. Think of it less like copying and more like picking something up and putting it down elsewhere, or just sticking a new label on it.

Moving Files and Directories

The syntax is similar to `cp`: `mv source destination`. If the destination is an existing directory, the source file or directory is moved *into* it.

```
# Move a file into the backups directory
mv yet_another_copy.txt backups/

ls
# yet_another_copy.txt should be gone from here

ls backups/
# yet_another_copy.txt should be here now
```

You can move multiple items at once:

```
# Let's move my_first_file.txt as well
mv my_first_file.txt backups/
ls backups/
```

Unlike `cp`, you don't typically need a special option like -r to move directories. `mv` handles directories just fine.

```
# Create another directory
mkdir temporary_stuff

# Move it into backups
mv temporary_stuff backups/

ls backups/
```

You should now see `temporary_stuff` inside the `backups` directory.

Renaming Files and Directories

This is where mv does double duty. If the `destination` argument is *not* an existing directory, mv assumes you want to rename the `source`.

```
# Rename report.log to activity.log
mv report.log activity.log

ls
# report.log is gone, activity.log is present
```

This works for directories too:

```
# Rename backups_copy to old_backups
mv backups_copy old_backups

ls
# backups_copy is gone, old_backups is present
```

It feels intuitive: moving something *onto* a new name is essentially renaming it.

Just like cp, mv can potentially overwrite files if the target name already exists. Use the -i (interactive) option to be prompted before overwriting:

```
# Create a dummy file
touch important_file.txt

# Try to rename activity.log to important_file.txt interactively
mv -i activity.log important_file.txt

mv: overwrite 'important_file.txt'?
```

And -v (verbose) works here too, showing you the move or rename operation:

```
mv -v important_file.txt config.ini

renamed 'important_file.txt' -> 'config.ini'
```

Removing Files: rm

Now we come to rm (remove). This command deletes files. Simple as that. But **be extremely careful** with rm. Unlike deleting files in most graphical environments, **there**

is no Recycle Bin or Trash Can on the standard Linux command line. Once you rm a file, it's generally gone for good (barring advanced data recovery techniques, which are beyond our scope).

To remove a file, just provide its name:

```
# Let's remove the copy we made earlier
rm copy_of_original.txt

ls
# copy_of_original.txt should be gone
```

You can remove multiple files at once:

```
# Clean up some of our practice files
rm data.csv notes_for_meeting config.ini

ls
# Only original.txt and activity.log (if you kept it) should remain
# outside the directories
```

Because rm is permanent, it's highly recommended, especially when learning, to use the -i (interactive) option. This will prompt you for confirmation before deleting each file:

```
touch file_a file_b file_c
rm -i file_a file_b file_c


rm: remove regular empty file 'file_a'? y
rm: remove regular empty file 'file_b'? y
rm: remove regular empty file 'file_c'? n
```

Now, what about files you might not have permission to write to, or other situations where the system might normally ask for confirmation? The -f (force) option tells rm to remove files without prompting, even if they are write-protected (as long as you own the file or have permission in the directory). It also suppresses errors if a file doesn't exist.

Use rm -f with extreme caution. It overrides the safety net of -i. Combining -r (recursive, which we'll see next) and -f is particularly dangerous, as it can wipe out entire directory structures silently and instantly. Always double-check commands involving rm -f or rm -rf before pressing Enter.

Removing Empty Directories: `rmdir`

If you want to remove a directory, but *only* if it's empty, you can use `rmdir` (remove directory).

```
# Create an empty directory
mkdir empty_dir

# Remove it
rmdir empty_dir

# Verify it's gone
ls
```

If you try to use `rmdir` on a directory that contains files or subdirectories, it will fail:

```
# Try removing the non-empty 'old_backups' directory
rmdir old_backups

rmdir: failed to remove 'old_backups': Directory not empty
```

This makes `rmdir` a relatively safe command, as it won't let you accidentally delete a directory that still has contents.

Removing Directories and Their Contents: `rm -r`

So, how *do* you remove a directory that isn't empty? You use `rm` with the `-r` (recursive) option, the same one we used with `cp`.

```
# Remove the old_backups directory and everything inside it
rm -r old_backups

# Verify it's gone
ls
```

This is the command that demands the most respect and caution. `rm -r` will dive into the specified directory and delete *everything* inside it – files, subdirectories, files within subdirectories, and so on – before finally removing the directory itself.

Combining -r with -f gives you rm -rf, which recursively forces deletion without any prompts. While powerful for cleaning up complex structures quickly, a small typo in an rm -rf command can have catastrophic consequences, potentially deleting critical system files or your personal data.

Always, always, always double-check your rm -r **and especially** rm -rf **commands before you hit Enter.** Using the -i option along with -r (rm -ri directory_name) can add a layer of safety by prompting for each item, but it can be tedious for large directories.

A common piece of advice is to ls the target directory first (ls directory_name) to make sure you know what's inside before you rm -r it.

Chapter Summary

You've now added some serious tools to your command-line toolkit! We learned how to create directories with mkdir (and its handy -p option for parents), create empty files or update timestamps with touch, duplicate files and directories using cp (remembering -r for directories and -i for safety), and move or rename items with mv. Most importantly, we covered removing files with rm and empty directories with rmdir. We paid special attention to the power and potential danger of rm -r for deleting directories and their contents, stressing the need for caution due to the lack of an undelete feature.

You can now create, organize, and clean up your filesystem structure. But what about actually looking *inside* the files you've created and copied? In the next chapter, we'll explore commands like cat, less, head, and tail to view the contents of your text files directly from the command line.

Chapter 4: Viewing File Contents

In the last chapter, you became a filesystem architect, learning to create, copy, move, and remove files and directories. You've got the structure sorted, but what about the actual *content* inside those files? Often, you'll need to peek inside a configuration file, read a log, check the output of a script, or just remind yourself what's in that notes.txt you created. This chapter focuses on the command-line tools designed specifically for viewing file contents without necessarily opening them in a full editor. We'll cover `cat` for displaying whole files, `less` and `more` for reading page by page, `head` and `tail` for looking at the beginning or end, and `file` for figuring out what kind of data a file actually holds. Let's start reading!

Displaying Entire Files: `cat`

The `cat` command is perhaps the simplest way to view a file's content. Its name comes from "con**cat**enate," and while it *can* be used to join files together (which we'll touch on), its most common basic use is just dumping the entire content of a single file to your terminal screen (standard output).

Let's create a sample file first. We'll use a command called `echo` along with output redirection (>), which you'll learn more about in Chapter 9. For now, just know this creates a file named poem.txt with three lines of text:

```
echo "Roses are red," > poem.txt
echo "Violets are blue," >> poem.txt
echo "Linux is awesome, and so are you!" >> poem.txt
# The >> appends lines instead of overwriting
```

Now, use `cat` to display it:

```
cat poem.txt
```

The output will be the exact content of the file:

```
Roses are red,
Violets are blue,
Linux is awesome, and so are you!
```

Simple, right? cat reads the file from beginning to end and prints it all out. You can also give cat multiple filenames, and it will display them one after the other, concatenating their content on the output:

```
# Create another small file
echo "--- End of poem ---" > separator.txt

# Cat both files
cat poem.txt separator.txt

Roses are red,
Violets are blue,
Linux is awesome, and so are you!
--- End of poem ---
```

A useful option for cat is -n, which adds line numbers to the output:

```
cat -n poem.txt

     1  Roses are red,
     2  Violets are blue,
     3  Linux is awesome, and so are you!
```

Now, for the **potential pitfalls**: cat is great for short text files. However, if you use cat on a very long file (like a large log file), it will dump *all* of its content to your terminal as fast as it can. This will likely scroll past your screen way too quickly for you to read anything useful. Even worse, if you accidentally cat a binary file (like an executable program or an image), it will spew unintelligible garbage characters to your terminal, potentially messing up its display settings until you reset it.

Think of cat like unrolling an entire ancient scroll onto the floor. It's fine if the scroll is short, but impractical and messy if it's hundreds of feet long or written in an alien language. Use cat primarily for quickly viewing small text files or when you specifically want to combine files. For exploring larger files, we need a better tool.

Viewing Files Page by Page: less

When a file is too long to fit on one screen, you need a **pager** – a program that displays content one screenful (or "page") at a time, allowing you to navigate through it. The most common and versatile pager on modern Linux systems is less.

Let's try it on a longer file. Most Linux systems have a text file containing a dictionary. Let's find one (its exact location might vary, /usr/share/dict/words is common) and view it with less:

```
# The exact path might differ on your system
less /usr/share/dict/words
```

Instead of the whole file rushing past, less will display only the first screenful of text, usually with a colon (:) or the filename at the bottom, indicating it's waiting for your input.

```
A
a
aa
aal
aalii
aam
Aani
aardvark
aardwolf
Aaron
Aaronic
Aaronical
Aaronite
Aaronitic
Aaru
Ab
aba
/usr/share/dict/words
```

(Your dictionary file might look different)

Now you can navigate! Here are the essential keys for moving within less:

- **Scroll Down:**

- Spacebar or `PageDown`: Move down one full screen.
- `Enter` or `Down Arrow`: Move down one line.
- **Scroll Up:**
  - `b` or `PageUp`: Move up one full screen.
  - `Up Arrow`: Move up one line.
- **Go To:**
  - `g`: Go to the beginning of the file.
  - `G`: Go to the end of the file.
- **Search:**
  - `/` followed by text (e.g., `/linux`): Search *forward* for the text. Press Enter to start searching.
  - `?` followed by text (e.g., `?kernel`): Search *backward* for the text. Press Enter.
  - `n`: Go to the *next* match (in the same direction you were searching).
  - `N`: Go to the *previous* match (in the opposite direction).
- **Quit:**
  - `q`: Exit `less` and return to your shell prompt.

`less` **is incredibly useful** because, unlike its predecessor `more`, it allows you to scroll both forward and backward easily. It doesn't need to read the entire file into memory before displaying it, making it efficient even for enormous files. Get comfortable with `less`; it's your go-to tool for exploring file contents interactively.

The Older Pager: `more`

Before `less`, there was `more`. It functions similarly by displaying text one screenful at a time, pausing with `--More--` at the bottom.

```
more /usr/share/dict/words
```

You primarily navigate forward using the `Spacebar` (next screen) or `Enter` (next line). Searching (`/`) usually works too. However, `more`'s biggest limitation is that **scrolling backward is generally not supported** or is very limited. Once you've paged forward, you usually can't go back up easily.

Why mention `more`? Because `less` is generally preferred ("less is more," as the saying goes, ironically), you might occasionally encounter very old UNIX systems or minimal Linux installations where `less` isn't available, but `more` likely is. It's good to know it exists, but you'll probably use `less` 99% of the time.

Peeking at the Beginning: head

Sometimes, you don't need to see the whole file or page through it; you just want a quick look at the very first few lines. This is often useful for checking header information in data files or the beginning of scripts. The head command does exactly this.

By default, head shows the first 10 lines of a file:

```
# Using our poem from before
head poem.txt

Roses are red,
Violets are blue,
Linux is awesome, and so are you!
```

(Since our file is only 3 lines, it shows all of them)

Let's try it on the dictionary file:

```
head /usr/share/dict/words

A
a
aa
aal
aalii
aam
Aani
aardvark
aardwolf
Aaron
```

If you want to see a different number of lines, use the -n option followed by the desired count. You can also use a shorthand by just putting - and the number.

```
# Show the first 3 lines
head -n 3 /usr/share/dict/words
# Or equivalently:
head -3 /usr/share/dict/words

A
a
aa
```

head is simple, fast, and perfect when you only care about the start of a file.

Looking at the End: `tail`

Conversely, you often need to see the *last* few lines of a file. This is incredibly common when checking log files, as new entries are usually appended to the end. The `tail` command is designed for this.

By default, `tail` shows the last 10 lines:

```
# Create a slightly longer dummy log file
echo "INFO: Service started." > app.log
echo "WARN: Configuration value missing, using default." >> app.log
# ... add many more lines ...
for i in {1..15}; do echo "DEBUG: Processing item $i" >> app.log; done
echo "ERROR: Failed to connect to database." >> app.log
echo "INFO: Service shutting down." >> app.log


# View the last 10 lines
tail app.log


DEBUG: Processing item 7
DEBUG: Processing item 8
DEBUG: Processing item 9
DEBUG: Processing item 10
DEBUG: Processing item 11
DEBUG: Processing item 12
DEBUG: Processing item 13
DEBUG: Processing item 14
DEBUG: Processing item 15
ERROR: Failed to connect to database.
INFO: Service shutting down.
```

(Output adjusted slightly for clarity, showing 11 lines due to the structure)

Similar to head, you can specify the number of lines with -n or -count:

```
# Show the last 5 lines
tail -n 5 app.log
# Or equivalently:
tail -5 app.log


DEBUG: Processing item 13
DEBUG: Processing item 14
DEBUG: Processing item 15
```

```
ERROR: Failed to connect to database.
INFO: Service shutting down.
```

Following File Changes: -f

One of tail's most powerful features is the -f (follow) option. When you run tail -f filename, it displays the last few lines (10 by default) and then *waits*. As new lines are added to the file by another process, tail -f will automatically print them to your screen in real-time.

This is indispensable for monitoring log files or other actively changing files.

```
# Start following the log file (it will wait here)
tail -f app.log

DEBUG: Processing item 8
DEBUG: Processing item 9
DEBUG: Processing item 10
DEBUG: Processing item 11
DEBUG: Processing item 12
DEBUG: Processing item 13
DEBUG: Processing item 14
DEBUG: Processing item 15
ERROR: Failed to connect to database.
INFO: Service shutting down.
```

Now, open *another* terminal window (or run a command in the background using & if you know how) and append a line to the log:

```
echo "WARN: User login attempt failed." >> app.log
```

Switch back to the terminal where tail -f is running. You'll see the new line appear almost instantly:

```
DEBUG: Processing item 8
...
ERROR: Failed to connect to database.
INFO: Service shutting down.
WARN: User login attempt failed.  <-- *This line just appeared*
```

To stop tail -f from following, press Ctrl+C.

Determining File Types: `file`

In graphical environments, you often rely on filename extensions (`.txt`, `.jpg`, `.pdf`) to guess what a file is. In Linux, while extensions are often used by convention, they **don't actually determine the file type** as far as the operating system or most commands are concerned. You could name an image `my_picture.txt` or a script `do_stuff.doc`, and Linux wouldn't inherently care (though the programs trying to *use* those files might get confused!).

So, how do you reliably find out what a file *really* contains? Use the `file` command. It examines the beginning of a file, looking for specific patterns or "magic numbers" that identify known file types.

```
# Check our text files
file poem.txt
file app.log

# Check a command (which is an executable binary)
file /bin/ls

# Check a directory
file /home/your_user

# Check a compressed archive (if you have one)
# touch dummy; tar czf archive.tar.gz dummy; rm dummy
# file archive.tar.gz

# Check an image file (if you have one)
# file my_image.jpg
```

The output will vary depending on the file, but it gives you a much better description than just the filename:

```
poem.txt: ASCII text
app.log: ASCII text
/bin/ls: ELF 64-bit LSB executable, x86-64, version 1 (SYSV), dynamically
linked, interpreter /lib64/ld-linux-x86-64.so.2, for GNU/Linux 3.2.0,
BuildID[sha1]=..., stripped
/home/your_user: directory
archive.tar.gz: gzip compressed data, was "dummy", last modified: ..., os: Unix
my_image.jpg: JPEG image data, Exif standard: ...
```

`file` is a handy utility when you encounter a file with an unknown or misleading name and want to understand its actual format before trying to view or process it.

Chapter Summary

You've now learned several ways to look inside files without needing a full text editor. We saw `cat` for dumping entire small files or concatenating them, but recognized its limitations for large or binary files. For comfortable reading of longer files, the pager `less` is your best friend, allowing easy scrolling and searching. We briefly met its older cousin `more`. When you only need the beginning or end of a file, `head` and `tail` are efficient tools, with `tail -f` being particularly valuable for watching log files grow in real-time. Finally, `file` helps you identify the true nature of a file based on its content, not just its name.

Knowing how to view files is essential, but so is knowing how to get more information about the commands themselves. What if you forget an option for `ls` or want to know more about what `tail` can do? In the next chapter, we'll explore the built-in help systems within Linux, primarily the `man` pages, so you can become self-sufficient in learning about any command.

Chapter 5: Getting Help When You Need It

You've learned a fair number of commands already, from navigating (cd, ls, pwd) to managing files (mkdir, cp, mv, rm) and viewing their contents (cat, less, head, tail). That's excellent progress! However, the Linux command line offers thousands of commands, each often with dozens of options (remember those -l, -a, -r flags we saw back in Chapters 2 and 3?). Nobody remembers everything all the time, not even seasoned veterans. The *real* skill isn't memorizing every single detail, but knowing **how to find the information you need when you need it**. Thankfully, Linux comes equipped with excellent built-in help systems. This chapter is your guide to using these resources, turning moments of "How do I do that again?" into opportunities for learning.

The Manual Pages: man

The primary, most traditional, and often most comprehensive source of documentation on a Linux system is the **manual pages**, commonly known as **man pages**. Think of them as the official instruction manuals for nearly every command, system call (a way programs talk to the kernel), and configuration file format. The command to access them is simple: man.

Accessing Manual Pages

To view the manual page for a specific command, just type man followed by the command name. Let's look up the manual for ls, a command we used extensively in Chapter 2:

```
man ls
```

Your screen will clear, and you'll be presented with the manual page for ls, likely displayed using the less pager we learned about in Chapter 4.

```
LS(1)                          User Commands                          LS(1)

NAME
       ls - list directory contents

SYNOPSIS
       ls [OPTION]... [FILE]...

DESCRIPTION
       List information about the FILEs (the current directory by default).
       Sort entries alphabetically if none of -cftuvSUX nor --sort is speci-
       fied.

       Mandatory arguments to long options are mandatory for short options
       too.

       -a, --all
              do not ignore entries starting with .

       -A, --almost-all
              do not list implied . and ..

       --author
              with -l, print the author of each file

       -b, --escape
              print C-style escapes for nongraphic characters

       --block-size=SIZE
              with -l, scale sizes by SIZE when printing them; e.g.,
              '--block-size=M'; see SIZE format below

 Manual page ls(1) line 1 (press h for help or q to quit)
```

(The exact output might vary slightly based on your ls *version and system.)*

You see the command name, a brief description, how to use it (the SYNOPSIS), and then a long list of options.

Navigating Man Pages

Since man typically uses less to display the pages, you navigate them exactly as you learned in Chapter 4:

- **Scroll Down:** Spacebar (page), Enter (line), Down Arrow (line)
- **Scroll Up:** b (page), Up Arrow (line)
- **Search:** / then text (forward), ? then text (backward), n (next match), N (previous match)
- **Quit:** q

Feel free to scroll down the ls man page. You'll find detailed explanations for options like -l, -a, -h, -r, and many, many more. It's the definitive reference.

Understanding Man Page Sections

Man pages are traditionally organized into standard sections to make information easier to find. While not every page has every section, you'll frequently encounter these:

Section	Content
NAME	The command name and a very brief (one-line) description of its purpose.
SYNOPSIS	Shows the command's syntax, including options and arguments. Square brackets [] usually indicate optional items. Ellipses ... mean "one or more".
DESCRIPTION	A more detailed explanation of what the command does.
OPTIONS	An alphabetical list of the command-line options (flags like -l, --help) and what they do. This is often the longest section.
EXAMPLES	Practical examples of how to use the command. Invaluable for learning!
FILES	Lists configuration files the command might use (e.g., /etc/someconfig).
EXIT STATUS	Describes the numeric codes the command returns upon exiting (useful for scripting, see Chapter 15). 0 usually means success.
AUTHOR	Who wrote the command or the man page.
REPORTING BUGS	Where to report problems found with the command.
COPYRIGHT	License information.
SEE ALSO	Lists related commands or man pages that might be helpful. A great way to discover related tools.

Don't feel obligated to read a man page from start to finish every time. Often, you'll jump straight to the **OPTIONS** section to remind yourself of a specific flag or browse the **EXAMPLES** to see how it's used in practice. The **SEE ALSO** section is particularly useful for exploring related functionality.

Searching Man Pages: `man -k` **(or** `apropos`**)**

What if you don't know the exact command name, but you know what you *want* to do? For example, maybe you want to find commands related to "copying files." You can search the NAME and short descriptions of all man pages using the `-k` option (for keyword).

```
man -k "copy file"
```

This will search the man page database and list any pages whose name or short description contains "copy file".

```
cp (1)                   - copy files and directories
cpio (1)                 - copy files to and from archives
dd (1)                   - convert and copy a file
install (1)              - copy files and set attributes
rsync (1)                - a fast, versatile, remote (and local) file-copying tool
scp (1)                  - secure copy (remote file copy program)
# ... possibly more results ...
```

This shows us `cp` (which we know from Chapter 3), but also introduces other related tools like `install`, `rsync`, and `scp` (which we'll see in Chapter 14).

An alternative command that often does the exact same thing as `man -k` is `apropos` (which is French/Latin for "concerning" or "regarding").

```
apropos "copy file"
```

You'll likely get the same output as `man -k`. Use whichever you find easier to remember. This keyword search is fantastic when you're exploring or trying to find the right tool for a job. *Note: The first time you run this, it might prompt you to build the search database, which is perfectly normal.*

The GNU Info System: `info`

While `man` pages are the traditional standard, many tools from the GNU Project (which provides much of the software in a typical Linux distribution, including Bash) use an alternative documentation system called **info**.

`info` documents are structured differently from man pages. They are organized as interconnected **nodes**, forming a hypertext system similar to web pages, but purely text-based. You typically start at a top-level node and follow links to sub-nodes containing more specific information.

Let's try viewing the info page for `ls`:

```
info ls
```

You'll enter the `info` browser, which looks different from man.

```
File: coreutils.info,  Node: ls invocation,  Next: dir invocation,  Up:
Directory listing

'ls': List directory contents
==============================

   The 'ls' program lists information about files (of any type,
including directories). Options and file arguments can be intermixed
arbitrarily, as usual.
...
* Menu:

* Which files are listed::        Which files 'ls' lists information for.
* What information is listed::     What information 'ls' lists for each file.
* Sorting the output::            How 'ls' sorts the files it lists.
* General output formatting::     How 'ls' formats its output in general.
* Formatting the file names::     How 'ls' displays individual file names.
...

--zz-Info: (coreutils)ls invocation, 41 lines --Top--------------------------
Welcome to Info version 6.7. Type C-h t for tutorial, m for menu item.
```

(Output is illustrative and may differ.)

Notice the "Menu" section with items like `* Which files are listed::`. These are links to other nodes.

Navigating Info Nodes

Navigation in `info` uses different keys than `less`:

- **Select Menu Item:** Move the cursor to a menu item (usually starting with `*`) and press Enter.
- **Next Node:** n (moves to the next logical node in sequence).
- **Previous Node:** p (moves to the previous logical node).

- **Up Node:** u (moves up one level in the hierarchy, often back to the menu you came from).
- **Top Node:** t (moves to the top-level node of the current info file).
- **Directory Node:** d (goes to the main info directory node).
- **Quit:** q

man **vs.** info

So, when do you use man and when info?

- man: Generally better for a quick lookup of a specific command's options or syntax. Its linear structure and familiar less navigation make it fast for reference. It covers a wider range of system items beyond just GNU tools.
- info: Often provides more tutorial-like, in-depth explanations, especially for complex GNU utilities (like the core utilities, GCC compiler, Emacs editor). The hypertext structure can be good for learning a tool comprehensively but can feel less direct for quick reference.

Many GNU tools have *both* a man page and an info page. The man page is often a summary or points you toward the info page for full details. Don't worry too much about which one to use initially; start with man, and if it seems too brief or suggests info, give info a try. You'll develop a preference over time.

Command-Specific Help: --help

Sometimes, you don't need the full manual or info page; you just need a quick reminder of a command's basic usage and its most common options. Many commands offer a built-in quick help summary via a --help option.

```
ls --help
```

This typically prints usage information directly to your terminal (it doesn't usually open less or info) and then exits.

```
Usage: ls [OPTION]... [FILE]...
List information about the FILEs (the current directory by default).
Sort entries alphabetically if none of -cftuvSUX nor --sort is specified.

Mandatory arguments to long options are mandatory for short options too.
  -a, --all                  do not ignore entries starting with .
  -A, --almost-all           do not list implied . and ..
```

```
        --author                 with -l, print the author of each file
    -b, --escape                 print C-style escapes for nongraphic characters
        --block-size=SIZE        with -l, scale sizes by SIZE when printing them;
                                   e.g., '--block-size=M'; see SIZE format below
    -B, --ignore-backups         do not list implied entries ending with ~
    -c                           with -lt: sort by, and show, ctime (time of last
                                   modification of file status information);
                                   with -l: show ctime and sort by name;
                                   otherwise: sort by ctime, newest first
    -C                           list entries by columns
... (many more options omitted) ...
Report ls bugs to bug-coreutils@gnu.org
GNU coreutils home page: <https://www.gnu.org/software/coreutils/>
General help using GNU software: <https://www.gnu.org/gethelp/>
For complete documentation, run: info coreutils 'ls invocation'
```

The output is usually much shorter than the man page, focusing on the syntax and a list of options. It's often the **fastest way** to check the spelling of an option or see the basic syntax.

Important Note: Not *all* commands support the --help option, although most GNU utilities and many other common commands do. If command --help gives an error, your next stop should be man command.

Finding Command Locations: which **and** type

Occasionally, you might need to know *where* on the system a particular command's executable file actually resides. This can be useful for debugging PATH issues (the PATH is an environment variable listing directories the shell searches for commands, covered briefly in Chapter 11) or just understanding where software gets installed.

The which command searches the directories listed in your PATH environment variable and prints the full path to the *first* executable it finds with the given name.

```
which ls
which cp
which man
which python3 # If Python 3 is installed and in your PATH


/usr/bin/ls
/usr/bin/cp
/usr/bin/man
/usr/bin/python3
```

(Exact paths might differ on your system, e.g., /bin/ls *instead of* /usr/bin/ls*)*

If which doesn't find the command in your PATH, it usually prints nothing or an error message.

A related and often more informative command is type. type tells you how the shell would interpret a given command name. It can distinguish between different types of commands:

1. **External Command:** A standalone executable file found in the PATH (like what which finds).
2. **Alias:** A shortcut defined by you or the system (see Chapter 11).
3. **Shell Builtin:** A command handled directly by the shell itself for efficiency (like cd).
4. **Function:** A shell function (more advanced scripting, see Chapter 15).
5. **Keyword:** A reserved word in the shell language (like if or for).

Let's try type on a few examples:

```
type ls

ls is hashed (/usr/bin/ls)
```

*(*hashed *means the shell has remembered its location for speed)*

```
type cp

cp is /usr/bin/cp

type cd

cd is a shell builtin
```

(See? cd *isn't an external program)*

```
# Many systems define 'll' as an alias for 'ls -l' or similar
type ll

ll is aliased to `ls -alF'
```

(Your alias might be different)

```
type if

if is a shell keyword
```

type gives you a clearer picture than which by revealing if a command is an alias or a built-in, which which wouldn't show.

Online Resources and Communities

The built-in help systems (man, info, --help) are powerful, but they aren't your only resources. The internet is teeming with information:

- **Search Engines:** Often, simply searching the web for "linux command to do X" or "man page for Y" will yield excellent tutorials, blog posts, and forum discussions.
- **Distribution Documentation:** Most major Linux distributions (like Ubuntu, Fedora, Debian, Arch Linux) have extensive online documentation, wikis, and manuals specific to their setup.
- **Q&A Sites:** Websites like Stack Overflow and its sister sites (Ask Ubuntu, Unix & Linux Stack Exchange) are invaluable. Chances are, someone has already asked (and gotten answers to) the very question you have. Learn to search these sites effectively.
- **Tutorial Websites:** Numerous websites offer tutorials on Linux and specific commands, often with more examples than man pages.
- **Community Forums/Chat:** Many distributions and open-source projects have dedicated forums or real-time chat channels (like IRC or Matrix) where users help each other.

While online resources are great, try to leverage the built-in help first. It's faster, always available offline, and specific to the exact versions of the commands installed on *your* system.

Chapter Summary

Forgetting command details is normal; knowing how to find help is essential. In this chapter, you learned how to consult the comprehensive **manual pages** using man, navigate them with less keys, understand their standard sections, and search them with man -k or apropos. We explored the hypertext info system, common for GNU tools, and learned its basic navigation. For quick reminders, the --help option provides a concise usage summary for many commands. We also saw how which and type can reveal the location and nature of a command. Finally, we acknowledged the vast wealth of online documentation and community support available.

You're now equipped not just to use commands, but to learn *about* them independently. This ability to find information is crucial as you progress. Now that you can manage files and get help, what about editing the *content* of those files directly from the command line? In the next chapter, we'll introduce simple yet powerful text editors like nano and take a first look at the legendary vim.

Chapter 6: Editing Text from the Terminal

So far, we've navigated the filesystem, managed files and directories, and learned how to view their contents using tools like cat and less. But what about *changing* the contents? While graphical text editors like Gedit, Kate, or VS Code are readily available on desktop Linux systems, there are many situations where you'll need or want to edit files directly within the terminal. Perhaps you're connected remotely to a server via SSH (as mentioned in Chapter 1 and detailed in Chapter 14), where a graphical interface isn't available. Maybe you're writing a script (Chapter 15) and want to make quick changes without switching windows. Or perhaps you just prefer the speed and keyboard-centric workflow of terminal editors. This chapter introduces two popular choices: nano, known for its simplicity, and vim, renowned for its power and efficiency (though it comes with a steeper learning curve).

Why Edit Text in the Terminal?

Before diving into the editors themselves, let's quickly recap why this skill is valuable:

1. **Remote Access:** When managing servers using SSH, the terminal is often your only interface. Knowing a terminal editor is essential.
2. **Configuration:** Many system configuration files (often found in /etc, as mentioned in Chapter 2) are plain text and are typically edited from the command line, sometimes requiring administrator privileges (which we'll cover in Chapter 7).
3. **Scripting:** When writing shell scripts or code directly on a Linux system, using a terminal editor keeps you in the command-line environment, streamlining your workflow.
4. **Efficiency:** For experienced users, terminal editors like Vim can be significantly faster for text manipulation than graphical editors, as operations are performed with keyboard commands instead of mouse movements.

5. **Availability:** Basic terminal editors are almost always available, even on minimal system installations where graphical tools might be absent.

Introducing nano: **A Simple Editor**

If you're new to terminal text editing, nano is an excellent place to start. It's designed to be intuitive, behaving somewhat like a simple graphical notepad but within your terminal window. It displays helpful command shortcuts directly on the screen, making it easy to learn the basics.

To edit a file (or create a new one if it doesn't exist), simply type nano followed by the filename:

```
# Let's edit the poem we created in Chapter 4
nano poem.txt
```

Your terminal will clear, and you'll see the contents of poem.txt loaded into nano's editing buffer. At the bottom of the screen, you'll see a list of common commands prefixed with ^ (which represents the Ctrl key) or M- (which represents the Alt key, or sometimes Esc depending on your terminal).

```
  GNU nano 6.2                      poem.txt
Roses are red,
Violets are blue,
Linux is awesome, and so are you!



















^G Get Help  ^O Write Out ^W Where Is  ^K Cut Text  ^J Justify   ^C Cur Pos
^X Exit      ^R Read File ^\ Replace   ^U Uncut Text^T To Spell  ^_ Go To Line
```

(Your nano version and screen might look slightly different.)

Basic Operations in nano

- **Navigation:** Use the standard arrow keys (Up, Down, Left, Right), PageUp, PageDown, Home, and End keys to move the cursor around the text, just like in most text editors.
- **Editing:** Simply start typing to insert text at the cursor position. Use the Backspace key to delete characters before the cursor and the Delete key (if available) to delete characters under or after the cursor.
- **Saving (Write Out):** To save your changes, press Ctrl+O ("Write Out"). Nano will prompt you for the filename to save to (it defaults to the current filename). Just press Enter to confirm. If you opened a new, unnamed file, you'll need to type a name here.
- **Exiting:** To exit nano, press Ctrl+X. If you have unsaved changes, nano will ask if you want to save the modified buffer. Press Y for Yes (you'll then be prompted for the filename if needed), N for No (discard changes), or Ctrl+C to cancel the exit command.
- **Searching (Where Is):** Press Ctrl+W to search for text. Type your search term and press Enter. Nano will move the cursor to the first match. You can press Alt+W (or Esc then W) to find the next occurrence.
- **Cutting and Pasting:**
    - To cut the entire line the cursor is on, press Ctrl+K ("Cut Text"). You can press it multiple times to cut consecutive lines. These lines are stored in nano's internal "cut buffer."
    - To paste the text you just cut, move the cursor to the desired location and press Ctrl+U ("Uncut Text").

nano has more features, like text justification (Ctrl+J), replacing text (Ctrl+\), going to a specific line number (Ctrl+_), and reading another file into the current one (Ctrl+R). You can always press Ctrl+G ("Get Help") to view nano's built-in help documentation (use Ctrl+X to exit the help screen).

The key takeaway for nano is its **simplicity and discoverability**. The most common commands are always displayed at the bottom, making it much less intimidating than other terminal editors for beginners.

A Glimpse into `vim` (Vi IMproved)

Now, let's switch gears and look at `vim`. Vim stands for "Vi IMproved," being an enhanced version of the classic UNIX editor `vi`. Vim is incredibly powerful, efficient, and available on virtually every Linux and UNIX-like system. Many experienced developers and system administrators swear by it. However, it operates very differently from editors like `nano` or typical graphical editors, presenting a significant learning curve for newcomers. The core concept you must grasp is its **modal nature**.

Understanding Vim's Modes

Unlike most editors where typing letters immediately inserts them into the text, Vim operates in several distinct *modes*. The main ones you need to know initially are:

1. **Normal Mode:** This is the default mode when you start Vim or after you press the `Esc` key. In Normal mode, keys on your keyboard **do not** insert text directly. Instead, they act as commands for navigation, deletion, copying, pasting, and other manipulations. Think of it as a command center for editing your text.
2. **Insert Mode:** This is the mode that behaves like a "normal" text editor. When you're in Insert mode, typing letters inserts them into the file. You enter Insert mode from Normal mode using commands like `i`, `a`, or `o` (we'll see these shortly).
3. **Command-Line Mode:** You enter this mode from Normal mode by typing a colon (`:`). This moves the cursor to the bottom of the screen, allowing you to type more complex commands, like saving (`:w`), quitting (`:q`), searching, or replacing text. After executing the command (by pressing `Enter`), Vim usually returns you to Normal mode.

This modal approach is what makes Vim initially confusing but ultimately very efficient, as you can perform complex edits without constantly moving your hands between the main keyboard and modifier keys or the mouse.

Getting Started with Vim

Let's try editing our `poem.txt` with Vim:

```
vim poem.txt
```

You'll see the file content, but notice you can't just start typing! You are in **Normal Mode**.

```
Roses are red,
Violets are blue,
Linux is awesome, and so are you!
~
~
~
~
"poem.txt" 3L, 75C                    1,1             Top
```

(The bottom line shows status information: filename, lines, characters, cursor position)

Basic Navigation (Normal Mode)

While the arrow keys often work in modern Vim configurations, the traditional (and often more efficient) way to navigate in Normal mode uses the keys h, j, k, l:

- h: Move cursor **left**
- j: Move cursor **down**
- k: Move cursor **up**
- l: Move cursor **right**

Why these keys? They are on the home row, meaning you don't need to move your right hand to navigate. Try moving around the poem.txt file using h, j, k, and l.

Entering Insert Mode

To actually start typing text, you need to switch from Normal mode to Insert mode. Here are a few common ways:

- i: Enter insert mode *before* the current cursor position.
- a: Enter append mode *after* the current cursor position.
- o: Open a new line *below* the current line and enter Insert mode there.
- O: Open a new line *above* the current line and enter Insert mode there.

Try moving your cursor somewhere in the middle of a line using h/j/k/l, then press i. You should see -- INSERT -- appear at the bottom of the screen. Now, whatever you type will be inserted into the text.

Getting Back to Normal Mode

This is crucial: **How do you stop inserting text and get back to command (Normal) mode?** Press the Esc key. The -- INSERT -- indicator at the bottom will disappear, and your keystrokes will once again be interpreted as commands. Make it a habit to return to Normal mode after you finish typing a piece of text.

Saving and Quitting (Command-Line Mode)

To save your work or exit Vim, you need to use Command-Line mode. First, make sure you are in **Normal Mode** (press Esc just in case). Then type a colon (:). The cursor will jump to the bottom line, waiting for your command.

- :w : **W**rite (save) the current changes to the file. Press Enter. Vim will confirm the write and you'll remain in the editor (in Normal mode).
- :q : **Q**uit Vim. This only works if you haven't made any changes since the last save. If you have unsaved changes, Vim will complain and refuse to exit.
- :wq : **W**rite (save) the changes *and* then **q**uit. This is very common.
- :q! : **Q**uit Vim and **discard** any changes made since the last save. The ! forces Vim to quit without saving. Be careful with this one!

Let's try it:

1. Enter Insert mode (e.g., press i).
2. Type some extra words.
3. Press Esc to return to Normal mode.
4. Type :wq and press Enter. Vim should save the file and exit back to your shell prompt. You can verify the changes using cat poem.txt.

Why Learn Vim?

Given the initial hurdle of modes, why do so many people invest time in learning Vim?

- **Efficiency:** Once mastered, text editing in Vim can be extremely fast. Complex operations become sequences of Normal mode commands executed without leaving the home row.
- **Ubiquity:** vi (the predecessor) or vim is guaranteed to be present on almost any UNIX-like system you encounter, even minimal installs or recovery environments. Knowing basic Vi/Vim ensures you can always edit a file.
- **Power:** Vim has a vast array of commands for text manipulation, searching (including regular expressions), running external commands, window splitting, scripting, and much more.
- **Customization:** Vim is highly configurable and extensible with plugins.

This section was just a tiny taste. Learning Vim is a journey. If you're intrigued, most systems have a command called vimtutor – running it launches an interactive tutorial within Vim itself, which is an excellent way to practice the fundamentals. Don't feel pressured to master it immediately; nano is perfectly adequate for many tasks. But knowing the basics of Vim is a valuable skill in the Linux world. Remember you can always use man vim (as covered in Chapter 5) to explore its extensive documentation.

Chapter Summary

In this chapter, we tackled the essential skill of editing text files directly from the command line. You learned why this is important, especially for remote administration and configuration. We started with nano, a user-friendly editor that's great for beginners due to its on-screen help and straightforward operation (using Ctrl key combinations like Ctrl+O to save and Ctrl+X to exit). Then, we took our first steps into the powerful but complex world of vim, understanding its core concept of **modes** (Normal, Insert, Command-Line). You learned basic navigation (h, j, k, l), how to switch between Normal and Insert modes (i, a, o, Esc), and fundamental Command-Line operations for saving and quitting (:w, :q, :wq, :q!).

You now have the tools to not only view files but also modify their content directly in the terminal. This opens up possibilities for changing configurations, writing notes, and starting simple scripts. With files created and edited, the next logical step is controlling who can access them. In Chapter 7, we'll delve into the critical concepts of Linux users, groups, and file permissions, which form the foundation of security and multi-user operation on Linux systems.

Chapter 7: Users, Groups, and Permissions

Linux, at its heart, was built from the ground up as a **multi-user** operating system, drawing heavily from its UNIX heritage. This means it's designed for multiple people (or processes) to use the system simultaneously, without interfering with each other's work or accessing things they shouldn't. How does Linux manage this separation and security? Through a system of user accounts, groups, and file permissions. In previous chapters, we learned to create and manage files; now, we'll learn how to control who gets to do *what* with them. Understanding these concepts is absolutely fundamental to using Linux effectively and securely.

Understanding Linux Users

Every action performed on a Linux system is done by a **user**. When you log in or open a terminal, you are operating as a specific user account. Each user has a unique username and typically belongs to one or more groups.

The Superuser: `root`

There's one special user on every Linux system: `root`. This user is often called the **superuser** or administrator. The `root` account has **unlimited privileges**. It can access any file, run any command, modify any system setting, and even completely break the system. Think of `root` as having the master key to every room and control panel in the entire building.

Because `root` is so powerful, logging in directly as `root` for everyday tasks is **strongly discouraged**. It's too easy to make a catastrophic mistake with a simple typo. A single misplaced `rm -rf` command (remember Chapter 3?) run as `root` could wipe out essential system files. Instead, you should perform daily work as a regular user and only gain `root` privileges when absolutely necessary for specific administrative tasks.

Regular Users

These are the standard accounts used for everyday work – writing documents, running applications, developing software, etc. Your personal account (like ada in our earlier examples) is a regular user account. Regular users have permissions to manage their own files (usually within their home directory, /home/username) but are restricted from modifying critical system files or accessing other users' private files unless explicitly granted permission. This separation protects users from each other and protects the system from accidental damage by users.

Checking Your Identity: whoami and id

We already met whoami back in Chapter 1. It simply prints your current effective username:

```
whoami

ada
```

A more comprehensive command is id. It shows your user ID (UID, a unique number assigned to your username), your primary group ID (GID), and all the groups you belong to.

```
id

uid=1000(ada) gid=1000(ada) groups=1000(ada),10(wheel),998(developers)
```

(Your specific UID, GID, and groups will likely differ. The wheel or sudo group often grants permission to use the sudo command, which we'll discuss next.)

Knowing which groups you belong to is important, as file permissions can be granted based on group membership.

Switching Users and Executing Commands

Sometimes, you need to perform actions as a different user, most often as root to perform system administration. There are two primary ways to do this: su and sudo.

Switching Users: su

The su command (substitute user or switch user) allows you to start a new shell session as a different user.

To switch to the `root` user, you typically type:

```
su -
# The '-' simulates a full login, setting up root's environment
```

You will be prompted for the `root` **user's password**. If you enter it correctly, your shell prompt will likely change, often ending in a # symbol instead of $, indicating you now have superuser privileges.

```
Password:
# whoami
root
# pwd
/root
```

You now have a full root shell. Every command you type runs with root privileges. To exit the root shell and return to your original user session, type `exit` or press `Ctrl+D`.

```
# exit
logout
$ whoami
ada
```

You can also use `su` to switch to another regular user (if you know their password):

```
su - otheruser
```

While `su` is functional, opening a full root shell is often considered less secure than necessary for many tasks. You might forget you're root and accidentally run a destructive command. For executing *single* commands with root privileges, `sudo` is generally preferred.

Executing Commands as Another User: sudo

The `sudo` command (superuser **do**) allows a permitted user to execute a *single* command as another user (usually `root`) without starting a new shell or needing the target user's password. Instead, `sudo` typically prompts for **your own** user password.

For example, let's say you need to edit a system configuration file `/etc/someconfig.-conf`, which requires root privileges. Instead of using `su`, you would use `sudo` with your chosen editor (like nano from Chapter 6):

```
sudo nano /etc/someconfig.conf
```

You'll be prompted for *your* password (ada's password in this case):

```
[sudo] password for ada:
```

If you enter your password correctly, and if your user account is configured to be allowed to use sudo (often by being a member of the sudo or wheel group), the nano editor will launch with root privileges, allowing you to save changes to the system file. Once you exit nano, you are immediately back to your regular user prompt.

Why is sudo preferred over su for many tasks?

1. **Security:** You don't need to know or share the root password. Users authenticate with their own passwords.
2. **Auditing:** sudo usage is typically logged (often in /var/log/auth.log or similar), providing an audit trail of who ran which administrative commands. su usage is logged too, but sudo logs the specific command executed.
3. **Granularity:** System administrators can configure sudo to allow specific users or groups to run only *certain* commands as root, rather than granting full root access. This configuration happens in the /etc/sudoers file (edited safely using the visudo command), which is a more advanced topic.
4. **Reduced Risk:** Running only single commands as root minimizes the window of opportunity for accidental destructive actions compared to operating in a full root shell.

Use sudo whenever you need to run a specific command with elevated privileges. Use su only when you genuinely need a persistent shell session as another user (which is less common for typical administration).

File Ownership

As mentioned, Linux is multi-user. To manage this, every file and directory in the Linux filesystem has **owners**. Specifically, each file/directory belongs to:

1. **One User:** The user owner, usually the user who created the file.
2. **One Group:** The group owner. By default, this is often the primary group of the user who created the file, but it can be changed.

Think of it like a document: one person might be the primary author (the user owner), but it might belong to a specific project team (the group owner).

Viewing Ownership

We saw this back in Chapter 2 when looking at the output of ls -l. Let's look again:

```
# Create a file in our practice directory (from Chapter 3)
cd ~/practice_files
touch sample_file.txt
ls -l sample_file.txt


-rw-r--r-- 1 ada developers 0 Jul 24 10:15 sample_file.txt
```

In this output:

- The **3rd column** (ada) is the **user owner**.
- The **4th column** (developers) is the **group owner**.

Ownership determines who has the rights to change the file's permissions and, by default, often gets preferential permissions (like write access).

Changing User Ownership: chown

The chown command (**change own**er) is used to change the user ownership of a file or directory. The basic syntax is chown new_owner filename.

```
# Let's assume another user 'bob' exists
# Try to change ownership of sample_file.txt to bob
# This will likely FAIL unless you are root
chown bob sample_file.txt


chown: changing ownership of 'sample_file.txt': Operation not permitted
```

Why did it fail? Because **only the root user can change the ownership of a file to someone else**. Regular users cannot give away their files (this prevents users from circumventing disk quotas or hiding illicit files under someone else's name).

If you *were* root (or used sudo), you could change the owner:

```
sudo chown bob sample_file.txt
ls -l sample_file.txt


-rw-r--r-- 1 bob developers 0 Jul 24 10:15 sample_file.txt
```

(Notice only the user owner changed)

You can also change **both** the user and group owner simultaneously using `chown user:group filename`:

```
# Change user to 'ada' and group to 'users'
sudo chown ada:users sample_file.txt
ls -l sample_file.txt


-rw-r--r-- 1 ada users 0 Jul 24 10:15 sample_file.txt
```

To change ownership recursively for a directory and all its contents, use the `-R` option:

```
sudo chown -R ada:users backups/
```

Changing Group Ownership: `chgrp`

If you only want to change the group owner, you can use the `chgrp` command (**change grp**). The syntax is `chgrp new_group filename`.

Unlike `chown`, a regular user *can* change the group of a file they own, but **only to a group they are a member of**.

```
# Assuming 'ada' is a member of 'developers' and 'users'
# Change group back to 'developers'
chgrp developers sample_file.txt
ls -l sample_file.txt


-rw-r--r-- 1 ada developers 0 Jul 24 10:15 sample_file.txt
```

If you try to change the group to one you're not a member of, it will fail (unless you are root).

```
# Assuming 'ada' is NOT a member of 'admins'
chgrp admins sample_file.txt


chgrp: changing group of 'sample_file.txt': Operation not permitted
```

Like `chown`, `chgrp` also supports the `-R` option for recursive changes on directories.

File Permissions Explained

Ownership is the first piece of the puzzle. The second, equally important piece is **permissions**. Permissions define *what* can be done with a file or directory, and by whom.

There are three basic permissions:

1. **Read (r)**: Allows viewing the contents of a file or listing the contents of a directory.
2. **Write (w)**: Allows modifying or deleting a file, or adding/removing files within a directory.
3. **Execute (x)**: Allows running a file as a program (if it's a script or binary) or entering (changing into) a directory.

These three permissions are defined for three categories of users:

1. **User (u)**: The actual user owner of the file.
2. **Group (g)**: Any user who is a member of the group owner of the file.
3. **Others (o)**: Everyone else (any user who is not the owner and not in the group).

Decoding `ls -l` Output

Let's revisit the first part of the `ls -l` output, often called the **mode string**:

```
-rw-r--r--
drwxr-xr-x
```

This string has 10 characters:

- **Character 1**: File Type (-=regular file, d=directory, l=symbolic link, etc.)
- **Characters 2-4**: Permissions for the **User** (owner) (rwx)
- **Characters 5-7**: Permissions for the **Group** (rwx)
- **Characters 8-10**: Permissions for **Others** (rwx)

If a permission is *not* granted, its place is marked with a hyphen (-).

Let's decode the examples:

- `-rw-r--r--` :

    - -: It's a regular file.
    - rw-: The **user** (owner) can read and write, but not execute.
    - r--: Members of the **group** can only read.

- r--: **Others** can only read. (This is a very common permission set for data files).
- drwxr-xr-x :
  - d: It's a **directory**.
  - rwx: The **user** (owner) can **read** (list contents), **write** (create/delete files inside), and **exec**ute (enter the directory).
  - r-x: Members of the **group** can **read** (list contents) and execute (enter), but cannot write (create/delete files).
  - r-x: **Others** can also **read** (list) and **execute** (enter), but cannot write. (This is a very common permission set for programs or shared directories you can enter but not modify).

Understanding permissions for directories is crucial:

Permission	On a File	On a Directory
Read (r)	View contents	List contents (ls)
Write (w)	Modify/delete file	Create/delete/rename files *within* the dir
Execute (x)	Run as program	Enter the directory (cd), access files inside

Notice that to *access* a file within a directory, you need execute (x) permission on the directory itself, even if you have read permission on the file! Think of x on a directory as the permission to "open the door" to that directory. Also, write permission (w) on a directory lets you create/delete files *in* it, regardless of the permissions on the files themselves (though you still need write permission on the file to *modify* its contents).

Changing Permissions: chmod

How do you change these r, w, x flags? Using the chmod command (**change mode**). chmod offers two main ways to specify the permissions you want: the symbolic method and the octal (numeric) method.

Symbolic Method

The symbolic method is often considered more readable because it uses letters. The format is chmod ˜**aapp** filename, where:

- **Who:** Specifies whom the change applies to:
  - u : User (owner)
  - g : Group
  - o : Others

- a : All (u, g, and o combined) (If omitted, it usually defaults to a but respects the umask, discussed later - it's often clearer to specify a).
- **Action:** Specifies what to do:
  - + : Add the permission.
  - – : Remove the permission.
  - = : Set the permissions *exactly* as specified (removing any others in that category).
- **Permission:** Specifies which permission(s) to affect:
  - r : Read
  - w : Write
  - x : Execute

Let's try some examples on our sample_file.txt (currently -rw-r--r--):

```
# Add execute permission for the user (owner)
chmod u+x sample_file.txt
ls -l sample_file.txt
# Output: -rwxr--r-- ...

# Remove write permission for the user
chmod u-w sample_file.txt
ls -l sample_file.txt
# Output: -r-xr--r-- ...

# Add write permission for the group
chmod g+w sample_file.txt
ls -l sample_file.txt
# Output: -r-xrwxr-- ...

# Remove read permission for others
chmod o-r sample_file.txt
ls -l sample_file.txt
# Output: -r-xrwx--- ...

# Set permissions for 'all' to read ONLY
chmod a=r sample_file.txt
ls -l sample_file.txt
# Output: -r--r--r-- ...

# Set user to rw, group to r, others to nothing
chmod u=rw,g=r,o= sample_file.txt
ls -l sample_file.txt
# Output: -rw-r----- ...
```

You can combine multiple specifications separated by commas. The symbolic method is great when you want to make specific incremental changes (add execute for the user) without affecting other existing permissions.

Octal (Numeric) Method

The octal method is faster to type once you understand it but can be less intuitive initially. It represents each set of permissions (user, group, others) as a single number, derived by summing the values for the granted permissions:

- **Read (r) = 4**
- **Write (w) = 2**
- **Execute (x) = 1**
- **No permission (-) = 0**

You combine these values for each category (User, Group, Others):

Permissions	Sum	Octal Digit
rwx	4+2+1	7
rw-	4+2+0	6
r-x	4+0+1	5
r--	4+0+0	4
-wx	0+2+1	3
-w-	0+2+0	2
--x	0+0+1	1
---	0+0+0	0

You then use a three-digit number with chmod, where the first digit represents User permissions, the second represents Group permissions, and the third represents Others permissions.

Let's set some common permissions using octal mode:

```
# Make a file readable/writable by user, readable by group/others
# Corresponds to -rw-r--r--
chmod 644 sample_file.txt
ls -l sample_file.txt


# Make a file readable/writable/executable by user, readable/executable by
group/others
# Good for scripts or directories you own
# Corresponds to -rwxr-xr-x
chmod 755 sample_file.txt
ls -l sample_file.txt
```

```
# Make a file readable/writable by user ONLY
# Good for private data files
# Corresponds to -rw-------
chmod 600 sample_file.txt
ls -l sample_file.txt

# Make a file executable by everyone (use with caution!)
# Corresponds to -rwxrwxrwx
chmod 777 sample_file.txt
ls -l sample_file.txt
```

The octal method sets the permissions *absolutely*. Unlike the symbolic + or -, it doesn't just modify existing permissions; it overwrites them completely with the specified numeric mode.

Both symbolic and octal methods achieve the same results. Use whichever feels more comfortable or appropriate for the task. Octal is common for setting initial permissions, while symbolic is often handy for targeted adjustments. Like chown and chgrp, chmod also supports the -R option for recursive changes.

Default Permissions: umask

When you create a new file (e.g., with touch or output redirection >) or a new directory (with mkdir), how does the system decide its initial permissions? It uses something called the **umask** (**u**ser file creation **mask**).

The umask is a value that is "subtracted" from the maximum default permissions to arrive at the initial permissions for new files and directories.

- The theoretical maximum permission for a new **file** is 666 (rw-rw-rw-). Files don't typically get execute permission by default for security reasons.
- The theoretical maximum permission for a new **directory** is 777 (rwxrwxrwx). Directories need execute permission to be usable.

You can view your current umask by simply typing umask:

```
umask
```

The output is usually a four-digit octal number, but for basic file permissions, we're primarily interested in the **last three digits**. A common default umask is 0022 or 0002.

Let's interpret 022 (ignoring the leading zero for now):

- The first 0 corresponds to special modes we aren't covering here.
- The second 2 corresponds to the **User** category.
- The third 2 corresponds to the **Group** category.
- The fourth 2 corresponds to the **Others** category.

The umask value represents the permissions to *remove*. A 2 in octal corresponds to w (write) permission. So, a umask of 022 means "remove write permission for group and others" from the default maximums.

- **New Files:** Default 666 (rw-rw-rw-) minus umask 022 (----w--w-) = 644 (rw-r--r--).
- **New Directories:** Default 777 (rwxrwxrwx) minus umask 022 (----w--w-) = 755 (rwxr-xr-x).

Let's test this:

```
# Assuming umask is 0022
touch new_file
mkdir new_dir
ls -ld new_file new_dir # Use -d for directory itself


drwxr-xr-x 2 ada developers 4096 Jul 24 11:30 new_dir
-rw-r--r-- 1 ada developers    0 Jul 24 11:30 new_file
```

The permissions match our calculation (644 for the file, 755 for the directory).

If your umask was 0002, only write permission for "Others" would be removed, resulting in 664 for files (rw-rw-r--) and 775 for directories (rwxrwxr-x). A more restrictive umask like 0077 would remove all permissions for group and others, resulting in 600 (rw-------) for files and 700 (rwx------) for directories.

You *can* change your umask for the current shell session using umask new_value (e.g., umask 0077), but the default umask is usually set in system-wide or user-specific shell startup files (like .bashrc, which we'll encounter in Chapter 11).

Understanding the umask helps explain why your newly created files and directories get the permissions they do.

Chapter Summary

This chapter covered the cornerstones of Linux's multi-user security model. We learned about user accounts, differentiating between the all-powerful `root` user and regular users. We saw how to check identity with `whoami` and `id`, and how to temporarily gain privileges using `su` (switch user) and, more preferably for single commands, `sudo` (superuser do). We then explored file ownership, understanding that every file belongs to a user and a group, and learned how to change ownership with `chown` and `chgrp`. The core of the chapter focused on file permissions: the read (`r`), write (`w`), and execute (`x`) permissions applied to the user, group, and others categories. You learned to decode the permission string in `ls -l` output and, critically, how to modify permissions using `chmod` with both the symbolic (letters) and octal (numeric) methods. Finally, we touched upon `umask` to understand how default permissions are assigned upon file creation.

Mastering users, groups, and permissions is crucial for working securely and collaboratively on Linux systems. You now have much finer control over your files. In the next chapter, we'll shift our focus from files on disk to the programs that are actively running on the system – processes – learning how to view, manage, and control them.

Chapter 8: Managing Running Programs (Processes)

We've spent the last few chapters mastering the filesystem – creating directories, managing files, controlling access with users, groups, and permissions (as discussed in Chapter 7). We're getting comfortable with the static elements stored on our disk. But a running computer is much more than just files; it's about the *programs* that are actively doing work, reading files, calculating data, or waiting for input. These running instances of programs are called **processes**. Understanding how to view, manage, and interact with processes is a vital skill for any Linux user, whether you're troubleshooting a slow system, stopping a misbehaving application, or controlling background tasks. This chapter is your introduction to the dynamic world of Linux processes.

What is a Process?

Think about a recipe in a cookbook. The recipe itself is like a **program** – a set of instructions stored on disk (a file). It doesn't *do* anything just sitting there. When you actually start following the recipe – gathering ingredients, mixing them, using the oven – that active execution of the recipe is like a **process**. It's the program *in action*.

A **process** is a running instance of a computer program. It has its own memory space allocated by the kernel, it consumes CPU time to execute instructions, and it can interact with system resources like files, network connections, and hardware devices. You can have multiple processes running the *same* program simultaneously (like cooking the same recipe in two different kitchens).

Each process on the system is assigned a unique identification number called the **Process ID** or **PID**. The kernel uses the PID to keep track of and manage every running process. We'll see PIDs pop up frequently as we explore process management commands.

Viewing Processes

The first step in managing processes is being able to see what's actually running on your system. Linux provides several commands for this, offering different perspectives.

Snapshot View: ps

The ps command (**process status**) gives you a snapshot of the running processes at the moment you execute it. It doesn't update in real-time; it just shows you what was happening when you ran the command. ps is highly flexible, but it has notoriously complex and somewhat inconsistent options due to historical reasons (merging different UNIX styles). We'll focus on two very common and useful invocations.

1. BSD Style (ps aux)

This style uses options without a leading dash. a shows processes for all users, u provides detailed user-oriented output, and x includes processes not attached to a terminal (like background services).

```
ps aux
```

The output can be quite long, showing every process running on the system. Each line represents one process, with several columns of information:

```
USER        PID %CPU %MEM    VSZ   RSS TTY      STAT START   TIME COMMAND
root          1  0.0  0.1 169692 11920 ?        Ss   Jul23   0:02 /sbin/init
splash
root          2  0.0  0.0      0     0 ?        S    Jul23   0:00 [kthreadd]
root          3  0.0  0.0      0     0 ?        I<   Jul23   0:00 [rcu_gp]
...
root        987  0.0  0.2 289400 16800 ?        Ssl  Jul23   0:01
/usr/lib/accounts-daemon
ada        1200  0.1  0.5 150000 45000 tty2     Sl+  Jul23   0:30 /usr/bin/gnome-
shell
ada        1530  0.0  0.1 210000 10000 ?        S    09:15   0:01
/usr/bin/pulseaudio --start
ada        2105  2.5  1.5 2500000 120000 ?      Sl   09:20   3:15
/usr/lib/firefox/firefox
ada        9125  0.0  0.0  14884  3840 pts/0    Ss   10:45   0:00 /bin/bash
```

```
ada        9150  0.0  0.0  17000  3100 pts/0    R+   10:48   0:00 ps aux
```

(Output is truncated and illustrative. Your PIDs and details will differ.)

Let's break down the key columns:

- **USER:** The username owning the process.
- **PID:** The unique Process ID.
- **%CPU:** Approximate percentage of CPU time the process has used recently.
- **%MEM:** Approximate percentage of physical memory (RAM) the process is using.
- **VSZ:** Virtual Memory Size (in kilobytes). How much memory the process has *asked* for.
- **RSS:** Resident Set Size (in kilobytes). How much physical memory the process is *currently occupying*. This is often a more practical measure of memory usage than VSZ.
- **TTY:** The controlling terminal associated with the process. ? usually means no controlling terminal (often a background service or kernel thread). pts/0 refers to a pseudo-terminal (like the one you're likely using).
- **STAT:** Process state (covered later). S=interruptible sleep, R=running, D=uninterruptible sleep, Z=zombie, T=stopped, +=foreground, s=session leader, l=multi-threaded, <=high-priority.
- **START:** The time the process started.
- **TIME:** The total accumulated CPU time used by the process.
- **COMMAND:** The command that launched the process, including arguments.

2. System V Style (ps ef)

This style uses options with a leading dash. e selects all processes, and f provides a "full" format listing, often including the parent process ID and showing the process hierarchy visually.

```
ps ef
```

The output structure is different, but contains much of the same information, plus the PPID:

```
UID        PID  PPID  C STIME TTY          TIME CMD
root         1     0  0 Jul23 ?        00:00:02 /sbin/init splash
root         2     0  0 Jul23 ?        00:00:00 [kthreadd]
```

```
root             3       2  0 Jul23 ?       00:00:00  \_ [rcu_gp]
...
root           987       1  0 Jul23 ?       00:00:01 /usr/lib/accounts-daemon
ada           1200     990  0 Jul23 tty2    00:00:30 /usr/bin/gnome-shell --
session ...
ada           1530    1200  0 09:15 ?       00:00:01 /usr/bin/pulseaudio --start ...
ada           2105    1200  3 09:20 ?       00:03:15 /usr/lib/firefox/firefox
ada           9125    1200  0 10:45 pts/0   00:00:00 /bin/bash
ada           9155    9125  0 10:52 pts/0   00:00:00  \_ ps ef
```

Key columns here:

- **UID:** User ID (the owner of the process).
- **PID:** Process ID.
- **PPID:** Parent Process ID. This shows which process started *this* process. Notice how ps ef (PID 9155) was started by bash (PID 9125). PID 1 (init or systemd) is the ancestor of most user processes.
- **C:** CPU utilization (often less granular than %CPU in ps aux).
- **STIME:** Start time.
- **TTY:** Controlling terminal.
- **TIME:** Cumulative CPU time.
- **CMD:** Command with arguments. The _ often indicates the process hierarchy.

Both ps aux and ps ef are valuable. aux gives good resource usage stats (%CPU, %MEM, RSS), while ef clearly shows the parent-child relationships (PPID). You'll likely use both depending on what information you need.

Dynamic Real-time View: top

While ps gives a snapshot, top provides a dynamic, real-time view of the processes running on your system. It refreshes automatically (usually every few seconds) and shows you which processes are currently consuming the most resources. Think of it as the command-line equivalent of the Task Manager in Windows or Activity Monitor in macOS.

Simply run:

```
top
```

Your screen will clear and display a continuously updating dashboard:

```
top - 11:05:30 up  1:20,  2 users,  load average: 0.05, 0.15, 0.10
Tasks: 250 total,   1 running, 249 sleeping,   0 stopped,   0 zombie
%Cpu(s):  1.5 us,  0.8 sy,  0.0 ni, 97.5 id,  0.0 wa,  0.0 hi,  0.2 si,  0.0 st
MiB Mem :   7800.0 total,   3500.0 free,   2800.0 used,   1500.0 buff/cache
MiB Swap:   2048.0 total,   2048.0 free,      0.0 used.   4500.0 avail Mem

    PID USER       PR  NI    VIRT    RES    SHR S  %CPU  %MEM     TIME+ COMMAND
   2105 ada        20   0 2500000 125000  80000 S   3.0   1.6   3:25.80 firefox
   1200 ada        20   0  150000  46000  30000 S   1.5   0.6   0:35.10 gnome-
shell
    987 root       20   0  289400  17000  10000 S   0.3   0.2   0:01.50 accounts-
daemon
      1 root       20   0  169692  12000   8000 S   0.0   0.2   0:02.10 init
      2 root       20   0       0      0      0 S   0.0   0.0   0:00.00 kthreadd
... (list continues and updates) ...
```

The output has two main parts:

1. **Summary Area (Top):**

   - Current time, uptime, logged-in users, system **load average** (a measure of system load over 1, 5, and 15 minutes).
   - **Tasks:** Total processes, and counts for running, sleeping, stopped, and zombie states.
   - **%Cpu(s):** Breakdown of CPU time usage (us=user, sy=system, ni=nice, id=idle, wa=I/O wait, etc.). High idle (id) is good!
   - **Memory/Swap Usage:** Statistics on physical memory (RAM) and swap space usage.

2. **Process List Area (Bottom):**

   - A list of currently running processes, typically sorted by CPU usage by default (most active processes at the top).
   - The columns are similar to ps aux (PID, USER, %CPU, %MEM, TIME+, COMMAND, etc.). PR (Priority) and NI (Nice value) relate to process scheduling priority. VIRT, RES, SHR relate to memory usage. S is the process State.

top is interactive! While it's running, you can use various single-key commands:

- q: Quit top.
- h: Display help screen showing available commands.
- k: Kill a process (it will prompt you for the PID and the signal to send).
- r: Renice a process (change its priority - requires privileges).

- f: Enter field management screen to add/remove/reorder columns.
- o: Change the sort order (e.g., type MEM after pressing o to sort by memory usage).
- spacebar: Force an immediate refresh.

top is invaluable for quickly identifying resource-hungry processes or getting a general feel for system activity.

An Enhanced View: htop (If available)

While top is standard and powerful, many users prefer htop. It's essentially a more colorful, user-friendly, and feature-rich version of top.

htop might not be installed by default on all systems. You can usually install it using your distribution's package manager (covered in Chapter 13):

```
# On Debian/Ubuntu based systems
sudo apt update
sudo apt install htop

# On Fedora/CentOS/RHEL based systems
sudo dnf install htop
```

Once installed, just run:

```
htop
```

You'll see a display that provides similar information to top but often includes:

- **Color:** Easier visual distinction.
- **CPU/Memory Meters:** Graphical bars at the top showing usage per CPU core and memory/swap.
- **Scrolling:** You can scroll vertically and horizontally through the process list using arrow keys or PageUp/PageDown.
- **Easier Interaction:** Use function keys (F1-F10) for common actions (Help, Setup, Search, Filter, Tree view, SortBy, Nice+, Nice-, Kill, Quit) - the available commands are usually listed at the bottom.
- **Tree View (F5):** Easily visualize the parent-child relationships between processes.
- **Mouse Support (Optional):** Often supports clicking on processes or column headers if your terminal allows it.

If htop is available, many find it a more pleasant and efficient tool than top for interactive process monitoring.

Understanding Process Information

Whether using ps, top, or htop, understanding the key pieces of information about each process is crucial:

- **PID (Process ID):** The unique number identifying the process. Essential for targeting commands like kill.
- **PPID (Parent Process ID):** The PID of the process that started this one. Helps understand process lineage (e.g., your shell starts the ps command).
- **USER / UID (User ID):** Who owns the process. Permissions often depend on this (as seen in Chapter 7). Processes generally run with the privileges of their owner.
- **%CPU / %MEM:** How much processor time and physical memory the process is consuming. Key indicators for performance issues.
- **STAT / S (State):** The current state of the process:
    - R (Running or Runnable): Actively using the CPU or ready to run as soon as the CPU is available.
    - S (Interruptible Sleep): Waiting for an event (e.g., user input, network data, timer). Most processes spend a lot of time sleeping.
    - D (Uninterruptible Disk Sleep): Waiting directly on I/O (usually disk). Processes in this state often cannot be killed easily, even with SIGKILL. Usually indicates a potential hardware or driver issue if persistent.
    - Z (Zombie): A process that has terminated, but its entry still exists in the process table because its parent process hasn't yet read its exit status. Zombies don't consume CPU or memory, but too many can fill up the process table. Usually, the parent process (or init/systemd) cleans them up quickly. Persistent zombies often indicate a bug in the parent process.
    - T (Stopped): Process execution has been suspended, usually by a signal like SIGSTOP (e.g., you pressed Ctrl+Z).
- **COMMAND / CMD:** The actual command line used to start the process. Helps identify what the process is doing.

Sending Signals to Processes: `kill`

Sometimes, you need to interact with a running process, perhaps to stop it, make it reload its configuration, or pause it. In Linux, you do this by sending **signals**. A signal is a notification sent to a process to alert it of an event.

The primary command for sending signals is `kill`. Despite its name, `kill` doesn't always terminate the process; it simply sends the specified signal. It's up to the process to decide how to handle most signals (though some, like `SIGKILL`, cannot be ignored).

The basic syntax is `kill [signal] <PID>`. You *must* know the PID of the process you want to signal.

Common Signals

There are many defined signals (you can see a list with `kill -l`), but these are the most common ones you'll use:

Signal Name	Number	Default Action	Common Use / Analogy
SIGTERM	15	Terminate	**Polite request to exit.** Allows cleanup. (Default for `kill`)
SIGKILL	9	Terminate (forcefully)	**Force quit.** No cleanup. Use as last resort. (Pulling the plug)
SIGHUP	1	Terminate	**Hangup.** Often used to tell daemons to reload config.
SIGINT	2	Terminate	**Interrupt.** Sent by `Ctrl+C`.
SIGQUIT	3	Terminate + core dump	**Quit.** Like `Ctrl+\`. Generates debug info.
SIGSTOP	19	Stop/Suspend	**Pause.** Cannot be caught/ignored. (Like `Ctrl+Z`)
SIGCONT	18	Continue if stopped	**Resume** a stopped process.

Note: The default action is what happens if the process doesn't specifically handle the signal.

Using `kill`

1. **Find the PID:** Use `ps`, `pgrep`, `top`, or `htop` to find the PID of the process you want to signal. Let's say we want to stop a hypothetical process `long_running_script.sh` with PID 5678.

2. **Send the Signal:**

- **Polite Termination (SIGTERM):** This is the default if you don't specify a signal. It's the first thing you should try.

```
kill 5678
# Equivalent: kill -TERM 5678 or kill -15 5678
```

Wait a few seconds and check if the process terminated using ps.

- **Forceful Termination (SIGKILL):** If the process ignores SIGTERM or is stuck (e.g., in state D), you may need to use SIGKILL. **Use this with caution**, as the process gets no chance to save data or clean up.

```
kill -KILL 5678
# Equivalent: kill -9 5678
```

- **Reload Configuration (SIGHUP):** Many server processes (like web servers or system daemons) are programmed to reload their configuration files when they receive SIGHUP, without needing a full restart. Check the specific daemon's documentation.

```
# Example: reload configuration for nginx (PID needs to be found
first)
# sudo kill -HUP $(cat /var/run/nginx.pid) # Example way to get
PID
sudo kill -HUP <nginx_master_pid>
# Equivalent: kill -1 <nginx_master_pid>
```

Finding and Killing Processes by Name: `pkill`, `killall`

Finding the PID with ps and then using kill can be a bit cumbersome. Linux provides convenient wrappers that let you signal processes based on their name or other attributes.

- pkill: Sends signals to processes matching a pattern. It's quite flexible. By default, it sends SIGTERM.

```
# Politely terminate all processes whose name contains 'firefox'
pkill firefox
```

```
# Forcefully kill all processes owned by user 'bob'
pkill -9 -u bob

# Send SIGHUP to processes named 'syslogd'
pkill -HUP syslogd
```

- **killall**: Similar to pkill, but often more specific, matching the exact command name. Behavior can vary slightly between systems. By default, it also sends SIGTERM.

```
# Politely terminate all processes named exactly 'bad_script.py'
killall bad_script.py

# Forcefully kill all 'apache2' processes
killall -9 apache2

# Ask interactively before killing each 'data_processor' process
killall -i data_processor
```

Word of Caution: Be careful when using pkill and killall with generic names. pkill python could potentially kill many different, unrelated Python scripts running on your system. It's often wise to first use pgrep (process **grep**) with the -l option to list the PIDs and names that *would* be matched, before using pkill or killall.

```
# See which processes match 'python'
pgrep -l python

# If the list looks right, then proceed
# pkill python
```

Background and Foreground Jobs

When you type a command in your terminal and press Enter, it usually runs in the **foreground**. This means the shell waits for the command to finish before giving you back the prompt ($). You can interact with the foreground process (e.g., provide input if it asks) but you can't type new shell commands until it completes or is stopped.

Sometimes, you want to run a command that might take a long time, but you want to continue using your shell immediately. You can run such commands in the **background**.

Running a Command in the Background: &

To start a process directly in the background, simply add an ampersand (&) at the end of the command line.

```
# Run sleep for 60 seconds, but return prompt immediately
sleep 60 &
```

The shell will print the **job number** (in square brackets, like [1]) and the **PID** of the background process, and then immediately give you back your prompt ($). The sleep command is now running independently in the background.

```
[1] 9320
$  <-- Prompt returned immediately
```

Viewing Background Jobs: jobs

How do you see which commands you've placed in the background in your *current* shell session? Use the jobs command.

```
# Assuming sleep 60 & is still running
jobs

[1]+  Running                 sleep 60 &
```

The output shows the job number ([1]), its state (Running), and the command itself. The + indicates the "current" job (the one that fg or bg would affect by default).

Bringing Jobs to the Foreground: fg

If you want to bring a background job back to the foreground (perhaps to interact with it or just wait for it to finish), use the fg (foreground) command, usually followed by % and the job number.

```
# Bring job number 1 to the foreground
fg %1
```

The command (sleep 60 in our case) will now take over the terminal again, and the shell will wait for it to complete. You won't get your prompt back until it finishes or you stop it.

```
sleep 60
(Terminal waits here until sleep finishes or is interrupted)
```

If you omit the job number (fg), it usually brings the most recent job (marked with +
by jobs) to the foreground.

Putting Jobs into the Background: bg (after Ctrl+Z)

What if you start a command in the foreground and *then* realize it's taking too long
and you want it to run in the background?

1. **Suspend the Foreground Process:** Press Ctrl+Z. This sends the SIGSTOP signal, which pauses the process immediately. The shell will usually print a message indicating the job is stopped and give you back the prompt.

   ```
   # Imagine you ran a long command:
   find / -name "*.log" > results.txt
   # Press Ctrl+Z while it's running
   ^Z
   [1]+  Stopped                 find / -name "*.log" > results.txt
   $ <-- Prompt returned
   ```

2. **Resume in Background:** Now that the job is stopped (check with jobs), you
   can use the bg (background) command (with the job number) to resume its
   execution *in the background*.

   ```
   bg %1
   ```

   The shell will confirm the job is now running in the background.

   ```
   [1]+ find / -name "*.log" > results.txt &
   $
   ```

The find command will now continue running, writing to results.txt, without
blocking your terminal.

Stopping Processes: Ctrl+C and Ctrl+Z Recap

These two key combinations are essential for interacting with foreground processes:

- **Ctrl+C:** Sends `SIGINT` (Interrupt) to the foreground process. Most programs interpret this as a request to terminate cleanly. This is the standard way to stop a command you started running in the foreground.
- **Ctrl+Z:** Sends `SIGSTOP` (Stop) to the foreground process. This pauses/suspends the process without terminating it. You can later resume it in the foreground (`fg`) or background (`bg`).

Chapter Summary

In this chapter, we shifted our focus to the dynamic aspect of Linux: running programs, or **processes**. You learned that a process is a program in execution, identified by a unique **PID**. We explored how to view processes using the snapshot command `ps` (with `aux` and `ef` options) and the real-time monitors `top` and the enhanced `htop`. We dissected the crucial information these tools provide, including PID, PPID, user, CPU/memory usage, and process state (`R`, `S`, `D`, `Z`, `T`). You learned how to interact with processes by sending **signals** using `kill`, `pkill`, and `killall`, understanding the difference between polite termination (`SIGTERM`) and forceful termination (`SIGKILL`), and other signals like `SIGHUP`. Finally, we covered managing **jobs** within your shell – running commands in the background (`&`), viewing them (`jobs`), and moving them between the foreground (`fg`) and background (`bg`) using `Ctrl+Z` to suspend.

You now have the ability to monitor and control the active components of your system. This is powerful! We've seen how commands produce output and how we can view files. What if we want to connect these commands and processes together, taking the output of one command and feeding it directly as input to another, or saving output directly to files? That's the subject of our next chapter, where we'll explore the indispensable concepts of redirection and pipelines.

Chapter 9: Redirecting Input and Output

You've become adept at running commands, managing files (Chapter 3), and even controlling running processes (Chapter 8). When you run a command like `ls` or `pwd`, where does the output actually go? By default, it appears right there in your terminal window. And when a command needs input (though we haven't seen many examples yet), where does it expect you to type it? Usually, your keyboard. These default pathways for information are incredibly important, and learning how to *change* them – to redirect the flow of data – is one of the most powerful concepts on the Linux command line. It allows you to save command output to files, feed files into commands as input, and chain commands together in incredibly useful ways. Get ready to become a data plumber!

Standard Streams Explained

Think of a running command (a process) as a little machine. To do its work, it often needs raw materials (input) and produces finished goods (output). Sometimes, things go wrong, and it produces error messages or waste. Linux standardizes these flows using three default **standard streams**:

1. **Standard Input (stdin):** This is where a process *reads* its input from. By default, it's connected to your **keyboard**. Its file descriptor number is **0**.
2. **Standard Output (stdout):** This is where a process *writes* its normal output to. By default, it's connected to your **terminal screen**. Its file descriptor number is **1**.
3. **Standard Error (stderr):** This is where a process *writes* its error messages or diagnostic output. By default, this is *also* connected to your **terminal screen**. Its file descriptor number is **2**.

Imagine a workshop machine: stdin (0) is the input hopper where you load materials (keyboard). stdout (1) is the conveyor belt carrying the finished products out (terminal screen). stderr (2) is a separate chute where defective parts or warning lights appear (also the terminal screen, by default).

Why are stdout and stderr separate, even if they both go to the screen? This separation is crucial. It allows you to redirect the *normal* output somewhere (like a file) while still seeing any *error* messages immediately on your screen, preventing errors from getting lost inside a data file.

Redirecting Standard Output (> and >>)

What if you don't want the output of a command to just appear on the screen? What if you want to save it to a file for later analysis, documentation, or use by another program? This is where output redirection comes in, using the > and >> operators.

Overwriting with >

The > operator redirects the **standard output (stdout)** of a command to a file. If the file doesn't exist, it's created. If the file *does* exist, **it gets overwritten without warning**.

Let's try saving the output of ls -l for our home directory:

```
# Make sure you are in your home directory
cd ~
ls -l > home_directory_listing.txt
```

You'll notice that nothing appears on your screen this time! The output didn't go to the terminal (stdout's default destination); it was redirected to the file home_directory_listing.txt. We can verify the file's contents using cat (from Chapter 4):

```
cat home_directory_listing.txt

total 48
drwxr-xr-x 2 ada ada 4096 Jul 20 10:00 Desktop
drwxr-xr-x 5 ada ada 4096 Jul 23 09:15 Documents
drwxr-xr-x 2 ada ada 4096 Jul 23 14:55 Downloads
-rw-r--r-- 1 ada ada  896 Jul 15 11:30 my_notes.txt
... (rest of your home directory listing) ...
```

Here's another example using echo (which simply prints its arguments to stdout):

```
echo "A line of text for the file." > my_data.txt
cat my_data.txt


A line of text for the file.
```

Now, let's run another `echo` command redirecting to the *same* file:

```
echo "This is a second line." > my_data.txt
cat my_data.txt


This is a second line.
```

Notice that the first line ("A line of text...") is gone! The second > command **overwrote** the original content.

Pitfall: This overwriting behavior is the most common source of mistakes with >. Always be careful when redirecting output to an existing file, as its previous contents will be lost unless you really intend to replace them. There's no undo!

Appending with >>

What if you want to *add* output to the end of a file without erasing what's already there? Use the >> operator. It redirects stdout and appends it to the specified file. If the file doesn't exist, it's created (just like >).

Let's build a simple log file using the `date` command:

```
# Add the current timestamp to log.txt (creates the file)
date >> system.log
cat system.log


Wed Jul 24 14:20:35 BST 2024
```

Now, let's append another timestamp a bit later:

```
# Wait a few seconds...
date >> system.log
cat system.log


Wed Jul 24 14:20:35 BST 2024
Wed Jul 24 14:20:55 BST 2024
```

The second timestamp was added to the end of the file. >> is perfect for creating log files or accumulating output from multiple commands into a single file.

Redirecting Standard Error (2>)

Okay, so > and >> handle standard output (file descriptor 1). But what about standard error (file descriptor 2)? If a command produces an error, that message still goes to your terminal by default, even if you redirect stdout.

Watch this: ls produces an error if you try to list a file that doesn't exist. Let's redirect the *standard output* of such a command to a file:

```
ls /etc/passwd /etc/non_existent_file > ls_output.txt
```

You'll see the error message appear directly on your terminal:

```
ls: cannot access '/etc/non_existent_file': No such file or directory
```

And if you check the output file, it only contains the *successful* output:

```
cat ls_output.txt

/etc/passwd
```

To redirect **standard error**, you need to explicitly specify its file descriptor number (2) before the > operator: 2>.

```
# Redirect only stderr to error.log
ls /etc/passwd /etc/non_existent_file 2> error.log
```

Now, the *successful* output appears on your terminal, because stdout wasn't redirected:

```
/etc/passwd
```

And the error message is now captured in error.log:

```
cat error.log

ls: cannot access '/etc/non_existent_file': No such file or directory
```

This is useful when you want to run a command or script and capture potential errors separately from the normal output, perhaps for later inspection or automated reporting. You can even redirect stdout and stderr to *different* files:

```
# Output goes to output.log, errors go to errors.log
some_command > output.log 2> errors.log
```

Redirecting Both Streams

Sometimes, you want to capture *everything* a command prints – both its normal output (stdout) and any error messages (stderr) – into a single file. There are two main ways to achieve this.

Method 1: The Traditional `> file 2>&1`

This is the classic, highly portable method that works in almost any Bourne-compatible shell (including Bash). It looks a bit cryptic at first:

```
ls /etc/passwd /etc/non_existent_file > combined_output.log 2>&1
```

Let's break down 2>&1:

1. `> combined_output.log`: This part redirects **stdout (fd 1)** to the file `combined_output.log`.
2. `2>&1`: This redirects **stderr (fd 2)** to the *same place that stdout (fd 1) is currently pointing to*. Since stdout is already going to `combined_output.log`, stderr gets sent there too.

The order is important! You must set up the stdout redirection *first*, then redirect stderr to wherever stdout is going. If you wrote `2>&1 > combined_output.log`, it wouldn't work as expected because stderr would be redirected to stdout's *original* destination (the terminal) *before* stdout gets redirected to the file.

Let's check the result:

```
cat combined_output.log
```

```
ls: cannot access '/etc/non_existent_file': No such file or directory
/etc/passwd
```

(Note: The order of lines within the file isn't always guaranteed)

Method 2: The Modern Bash Shortcut `&>`

Bash (and some other modern shells like zsh) provides a simpler shortcut to redirect both stdout and stderr to the same file: `&>`.

```
ls /etc/passwd /etc/non_existent_file &> combined_output_alt.log
```

This achieves the exact same result as `> file 2>&1` but is much easier to type and read. While convenient, remember it might not work in older or strictly POSIX-compliant shells. For maximum portability in scripts, `> file 2>&1` is often still preferred.

```
cat combined_output_alt.log

ls: cannot access '/etc/non_existent_file': No such file or directory
/etc/passwd
```

Redirecting to the Void: `/dev/null`

What if you want a command to run, but you don't care about its output *at all*? Maybe it's noisy diagnostic information you want to suppress, or you only care about its **exit status** (a concept important for scripting, see Chapter 15) to know if it succeeded or failed.

Linux provides a special "file" called `/dev/null`. Think of it as a black hole or a bottomless trash can. Anything redirected to `/dev/null` simply disappears forever.

```
# Discard standard output
noisy_command > /dev/null

# Discard standard error
error_prone_command 2> /dev/null

# Discard BOTH standard output and standard error
some_command &> /dev/null
# Or the classic way:
some_command > /dev/null 2>&1
```

This is very common in scripts to keep the output clean when you only need the command's side effects or exit code.

Redirecting Standard Input (<)

We've focused on output, but you can also redirect **standard input (stdin)**. Instead of a command waiting for you to type at the keyboard, you can tell it to read its input from a file using the < operator.

Many Linux commands can take a filename as an *argument* (cat file.txt, wc file.txt). However, some commands are designed *only* to read from standard input. Input redirection is essential for these, and it can sometimes be more efficient even for commands that accept filename arguments.

Let's use the wc command (**w**ord **c**ount). By default, wc -l counts lines from stdin until you signal end-of-file (usually Ctrl+D).

```
wc -l
# Type some lines
Line 1
Line 2
# Press Ctrl+D

    2  <-- Output showing 2 lines read from stdin (keyboard)
```

Now, let's use input redirection to make wc -l read from our poem.txt file (from Chapter 4):

```
wc -l < poem.txt

    3
```

The wc -l command didn't wait for keyboard input; its stdin (file descriptor 0) was connected directly to poem.txt, and it read the file's contents automatically, outputting the line count (3).

Another example using sort (which sorts lines of text):

```
# Create an unsorted list
echo "Charlie" > names.txt
echo "Alice" >> names.txt
echo "Bob" >> names.txt

# Sort the contents of names.txt using input redirection
sort < names.txt
```

```
Alice
Bob
Charlie
```

Here Documents (<<)

Sometimes, especially within shell scripts (Chapter 15), you want to provide several lines of input to a command without creating a temporary file. **Here Documents** allow you to embed multi-line input directly into your command or script.

The syntax is `command << DELIMITER`, followed by the lines of input, and finally the `DELIMITER` on a line by itself to signal the end. The `DELIMITER` can be any string, but `EOF` (End Of File) is very common by convention.

Let's feed multiple lines to `cat` using a here document:

```
cat << EOF
This is the first line supplied via a here document.
This is the second line.
It preserves spaces and formatting.
EOF
```

The output will be exactly the lines you typed between `cat << EOF` and the terminating `EOF`:

```
This is the first line supplied via a here document.
This is the second line.
It preserves spaces and formatting.
```

Here's the `wc -l` example again, using a here document instead of a file:

```
wc -l << MY_MARKER
Hello world,
this is input
for the wc command.
MY_MARKER

    3
```

Here documents are a powerful tool for embedding text blocks within scripts to feed into commands that expect input on stdin.

The Power of Pipes (|)

This is where things get really exciting. We've seen how to redirect input *from* a file and output *to* a file. But what if you want to take the standard output of *one* command and use it directly as the standard input of *another* command, without needing an intermediate file? This is achieved using the **pipe** operator: |.

Think of it as literally connecting a pipe from the stdout nozzle of the first command to the stdin funnel of the second command.

Command A | Command B

The shell runs both Command A and Command B concurrently. As Command A produces output on its stdout, the shell feeds that output directly into the stdin of Command B.

This allows you to build powerful **pipelines** by chaining together simple, specialized Linux commands. Remember the UNIX philosophy: "Write programs that do one thing and do it well. Write programs to work together." Pipes are the primary mechanism for making programs work together.

Let's see some examples:

1. **Paging through long output:** We saw `ls -l` can produce long output. Instead of redirecting to a file and then using `less` (Chapter 4), we can pipe `ls -l` directly *into* `less`:

   ```
   ls -l /usr/bin | less
   ```

   The output of `ls -l /usr/bin` doesn't flood your screen; it's fed directly to `less`, allowing you to page through it interactively.

2. **Filtering process lists:** Remember `ps aux` (Chapter 8) lists all processes? Let's find only the lines containing the word "firefox" using `grep` (a search tool we'll explore properly in Chapter 10):

   ```
   ps aux | grep firefox
   ```

   The entire output of `ps aux` is sent to `grep`, which filters it and only prints lines matching "firefox" to its stdout (which goes to your terminal). This is much more concise than saving `ps` output to a file and then searching the file.

3. **Counting files:** How many items are in `/usr/bin`?

```
ls /usr/bin | wc -l
```

ls /usr/bin lists the files (one per line usually, when piped). This list is piped to wc -l, which counts the lines it receives on stdin, effectively giving us the file count.

You can chain multiple pipes together:

```
# Find commands in history containing 'sudo', then count them
history | grep sudo | wc -l

# List files in /etc, sort them, then show the first 10
ls /etc | sort | head -n 10
```

Pipelines are a cornerstone of efficient command-line work in Linux. They let you combine simple tools in flexible ways to perform complex tasks succinctly, often avoiding the need for temporary files. Start thinking about how you can connect the output of one command to the input of another – it unlocks a whole new level of power.

Chapter Summary

This chapter illuminated the fundamental concept of standard streams: **stdin (0)** for input, **stdout (1)** for normal output, and **stderr (2)** for errors. You learned how to redirect these streams using powerful operators: > to send stdout to a file (overwriting), >> to append stdout, 2> to redirect stderr, and < to feed a file into stdin. We saw how to combine redirections, using > file 2>&1 or the modern &> file shortcut to capture both stdout and stderr, and how /dev/null acts as a data sink. You were introduced to **Here Documents** (<< DELIMITER) for providing multi-line input directly. Crucially, you discovered the **pipe (|)** operator, which allows you to connect the stdout of one command directly to the stdin of another, building powerful command pipelines.

You can now control the flow of information like never before! This ability to redirect streams and connect commands is essential for automation and complex data manipulation. We briefly used grep in our pipe examples. In the next chapter, we'll dive much deeper into tools specifically designed for finding things: searching for files across the filesystem with find and locate, and searching *inside* files for specific text patterns with grep.

Chapter 10: Finding Things

So far, you've learned to navigate, create, manage, view, and even edit files. You can redirect input and output and pipe commands together like a pro (Chapter 9). But what happens when you can't quite remember *where* you saved that important configuration file, or which script contains a specific function name? As your system grows and you create more files, finding what you need becomes a crucial skill. This chapter introduces the essential Linux tools for searching: `find` for powerful, detailed searches across the filesystem based on various criteria, `locate` for lightning-fast searches based on a pre-built database, and the indispensable `grep` for searching *inside* files for specific text patterns. Let's become digital detectives!

Searching for Files and Directories: `find`

Imagine needing to search every nook and cranny of a vast library for books matching specific criteria – published after a certain year, written by a specific author, or containing more than 500 pages. The `find` command is your meticulous librarian for the Linux filesystem. It searches through directory hierarchies in real-time, examining each file and directory it encounters against the criteria you specify.

The basic structure of `find` is:

```
find [path...] [expression...]
```

- `[path...]`: Specifies the starting directory (or directories) where the search should begin. If omitted, it defaults to the current directory (.). Common starting points include . (current directory), / (the entire system - use with caution, can be slow!), or ~ (your home directory).
- `[expression...]`: These are the tests and actions that `find` applies to each item it discovers. Expressions can include criteria for matching files (like name, type, size) and actions to perform on matching files (like print, delete, execute a command).

Let's explore some common expressions.

Searching by Name: `-name` and `-iname`

This is perhaps the most common use case: finding a file or directory by its name.

- `-name pattern`: Searches for files/directories with a name that *exactly* matches the `pattern`. This is **case-sensitive**. The pattern can include wildcard characters, but you often need to quote them to prevent the *shell* from expanding them before `find` sees them.

    - `*`: Matches zero or more characters.
    - `?`: Matches exactly one character.
    - `[]`: Matches any one character within the brackets (e.g., `[abc]`).
- `-iname pattern`: Same as `-name`, but the match is **case-insensitive**.

```
# Find all files named 'poem.txt' starting in the home directory
find ~ -name poem.txt

# Find all files ending with '.log' in the /var/log directory
# Need sudo for permissions in /var/log
# Quote the pattern to protect '*' from the shell
sudo find /var/log -name "*.log"

# Find files starting with 'sys' (case-insensitive) in /etc
find /etc -iname "sys*"

# Find files named exactly 'passwd'
find /etc -name passwd
```

The output will be a list of paths to the matching files or directories, each on a new line.

```
# Output for: find ~ -name poem.txt
/home/ada/practice_files/poem.txt

# Sample output for: sudo find /var/log -name "*.log"
/var/log/syslog.log
/var/log/auth.log
/var/log/kern.log
/var/log/dpkg.log
...

# Sample output for: find /etc -iname "sys*"
/etc/sysctl.conf
/etc/systemd
/etc/sysctl.d
```

```
/etc/syslog-ng

# Output for: find /etc -name passwd
/etc/passwd
```

Searching by Type: `-type`

You can restrict your search to only files, only directories, or other specific types using the -type expression followed by a character code. The most common types are:

- f: Regular file
- d: Directory
- l: Symbolic link

```
# Find only directories named 'backups' in the home directory
find ~ -type d -name backups

# Find only regular files ending in '.sh' (shell scripts) in the current dir
find . -type f -name "*.sh"

# Find all symbolic links within /usr/local/bin
find /usr/local/bin -type l
```

Searching by Size: `-size`

Need to find large log files that might be taking up space, or tiny configuration files? Use -size. The size is specified with a number followed by a unit suffix (or defaults to 512-byte blocks if no suffix). Common suffixes:

- c: Bytes
- k: Kilobytes (1024 bytes)
- M: Megabytes (1024k)
- G: Gigabytes (1024M)

You can specify exact sizes, or use + (greater than) or - (less than) prefixes before the number.

```
# Find files in /var/log exactly 100 kilobytes in size
sudo find /var/log -type f -size 100k

# Find files larger than 50 Megabytes in the home directory
find ~ -type f -size +50M
```

```
# Find files smaller than 1 Kilobyte in the current directory
find . -type f -size -1k
```

Searching by Time: -mtime, -atime, -ctime

You can find files based on when their data was last modified (-mtime), last accessed (-atime), or when their metadata (change time: permissions, ownership) was last changed (-ctime).

The time is usually specified in **days**. Similar to -size, you can use + (more than n days ago) or - (less than n days ago).

```
# Find files in /etc modified in the last 7 days
find /etc -type f -mtime -7

# Find files in your home directory accessed more than 30 days ago
find ~ -type f -atime +30

# Find files whose status changed exactly 1 day ago (yesterday)
find . -ctime 1
```

*Note: Some systems might mount filesystems with options (*noatime*) that disable accurate access time tracking for performance reasons.*

There are also -mmin, -amin, -cmin for searching by **minutes** instead of days.

Combining Criteria

The real power of find comes from combining these expressions. By default, find assumes an "AND" relationship – a file must match *all* specified criteria.

```
# Find regular files larger than 1MB modified in the last 3 days
# starting from the current directory
find . -type f -size +1M -mtime -3

# Find directories named 'config' owned by user 'ada'
find / -type d -name config -user ada 2>/dev/null # Redirect errors
```

(We added 2>/dev/null *to suppress permission denied errors when searching* /)

You can also use logical operators explicitly:

-   -a or -and (implicit default)

- -o or -or: Match if *either* expression is true.
- -not or !: Negate the following expression.
- ( ): Group expressions (often need quoting like \(\) to protect from the shell).

```
# Find files ending in .txt OR .md
find . -type f \( -name "*.txt" -o -name "*.md" \)

# Find files NOT owned by user 'root'
find /etc -not -user root
```

Executing Actions on Found Files: -exec and -delete

Simply listing matching files is useful, but often you want to *do* something with them. find provides several -action expressions.

- -print: The default action if no other action is specified. Prints the filename to stdout.
- -ls: Performs an ls -lids style listing for matched files. Useful for seeing details quickly.
- -delete: Deletes the matching files. **Use with extreme caution!** Always test your find command *without* -delete first to ensure it's matching only the files you intend to remove.
- -exec command {} \;: Executes the specified command on each matched file.
  - {} is a placeholder that gets replaced by the current filename being processed.
  - \; marks the end of the command. It needs to be quoted or escaped because ; has a special meaning to the shell.

```
# List details of all '.conf' files in /etc
find /etc -name "*.conf" -ls

# Interactively remove all files ending in '.tmp' in the current dir
# (safer than -delete for testing)
find . -name "*.tmp" -exec rm -i {} \;

# Change permissions to 644 for all '.txt' files in the practice_files dir
find ~/practice_files -name "*.txt" -type f -exec chmod 644 {} \;

# WARNING: Delete all files ending in '.bak' older than 30 days in home dir
# DOUBLE CHECK THE OUTPUT of find ~ -name "*.bak" -mtime +30 BEFORE running with
-delete!
```

```
# find ~ -name "*.bak" -mtime +30 -delete
```

A slightly more efficient variation of -exec is -exec command {} +. Instead of running the command once per file, this version appends multiple filenames to a single command invocation, which can be faster if the command supports multiple file arguments (like rm or chmod).

```
# Faster way to change permissions if many files match
find ~/practice_files -name "*.txt" -type f -exec chmod 644 {} +
```

find is incredibly versatile. Spend time with its man page (man find) to discover even more tests (like -user, -group, -perm) and actions. It's your go-to tool for complex, real-time filesystem searches.

Quick Database-Based Search: locate

While find searches the filesystem directly every time you run it (which can be slow, especially on large systems), locate takes a different approach. It searches a pre-built **database** of filenames and paths. This makes searching with locate extremely fast, often almost instantaneous.

To use it, simply type locate followed by the pattern you're looking for:

```
locate poem.txt
locate my_notes.txt
locate syslog

/home/ada/practice_files/poem.txt
/home/ada/my_notes.txt
/var/log/syslog
/var/log/syslog.1
/etc/syslog-ng
...
```

locate performs a simple substring match by default – if the pattern appears anywhere in the path, it's considered a match.

Updating the Database: updatedb

The catch with locate is that it only knows about files that were present when its database was last updated. If you create a new file, locate won't find it immediately.

100

The database is typically updated automatically on a schedule (often daily or weekly) by a background job running the `updatedb` command. However, you can manually update the database at any time (you usually need `sudo` privileges):

```
sudo updatedb
```

This process might take a few minutes as it scans the entire filesystem (respecting configuration rules about which paths to ignore). After `updatedb` completes, `locate` will be aware of any newly created or removed files.

`locate` vs. `find`: Pros and Cons

Feature	find	locate
Speed	Slower (searches filesystem in real-time)	Very Fast (searches pre-built database)
Accuracy	Always up-to-date	Only as accurate as the last `updatedb` run
Flexibility	Extremely flexible (search by size, time, perms, owner, type, execute actions)	Less flexible (primarily searches by name/path substring)
Resource Use	Can cause significant disk I/O during search	Minimal resource use during search (but `updatedb` uses resources)

Use `locate` when:

- You need a very fast search based only on filename or path.
- You're reasonably sure the file existed when the database was last updated.
- You're searching for system files or libraries whose locations don't change frequently.

Use `find` when:

- You need to search based on criteria other than name (size, time, permissions, type).
- You need to ensure the results are absolutely current.
- You need to perform actions (`-exec`, `-delete`) on the found files.
- The file might have been created very recently (since the last `updatedb`).

Both commands are valuable tools in your finding arsenal.

Searching Inside Files: `grep`

We've found files based on their names and properties. But what if you need to find files based on their *content*? Perhaps you remember a specific phrase in a configuration file but not the filename, or you need to find all log entries containing a particular error code. For searching *inside* files for text patterns, the `grep` command is indispensable. (`grep` stands for **g**lobally search for a **r**egular **e**xpression and **p**rint).

The basic syntax is:

```
grep [options] PATTERN [FILE...]
```

- `[options]`: Modify `grep`'s behavior (e.g., case-insensitivity, line numbers).
- `PATTERN`: The text string or regular expression you are searching for. It's often a good idea to quote the pattern, especially if it contains spaces or special characters.
- `[FILE...]`: The file(s) to search within. If omitted, `grep` reads from standard input (making it perfect for pipelines, as we saw in Chapter 9!).

Basic Text Searching

Let's search for the word "blue" in our `poem.txt` file:

```
grep "blue" poem.txt
```

grep will print every line from `poem.txt` that contains the pattern "blue":

```
Violets are blue,
```

If the pattern isn't found, `grep` produces no output.

You can search multiple files:

```
# Assume we have error.log from Chapter 9
grep "cannot access" error.log combined_output.log
```

The output will prefix each matching line with the name of the file it came from:

```
error.log:ls: cannot access '/etc/non_existent_file': No such file or directory
combined_output.log:ls: cannot access '/etc/non_existent_file': No such file or
directory
```

Common `grep` Options

`grep` has many options; here are some of the most useful:

- **-i (ignore case)**: Perform a case-insensitive search.

  ```
  grep -i "roses" poem.txt

  Roses are red,
  ```

- **-n (line number)**: Prefix each matching line with its line number within the file.

  ```
  grep -n "awesome" poem.txt

  3:Linux is awesome, and so are you!
  ```

- **-v (invert match)**: Select non-matching lines. Print lines that *do not* contain the pattern.

  ```
  # Show lines in poem.txt that DON'T contain "are"
  grep -v "are" poem.txt

  Linux is awesome, and so are you!
  ```

- **-r or -R (recursive)**: Search recursively through directories. When you specify a directory instead of a file, -r tells `grep` to search all files within that directory and its subdirectories.

  ```
  # Search for 'localhost' in all files under /etc (might need sudo)
  sudo grep -r "localhost" /etc
  ```

  This can produce a lot of output, showing the filename and the matching line for every occurrence found in the /etc hierarchy.

- **-w (word regexp)**: Only match whole words. For example, `grep -w "cat" file.txt` would match "cat" but not "catalog" or "concatenate".

- **-l (files-with-matches)**: Don't print the matching lines; just print the names of the files that contain at least one match. Useful when you just want to know *which* files contain the pattern.

```
grep -rl "bash" /etc
```

This would list the names of all files under /etc containing the word "bash".

Introduction to Regular Expressions (Regex) with `grep`

While `grep` can search for fixed strings, its true power comes from using **regular expressions (regex)**. A regular expression is a special sequence of characters that defines a search pattern. They allow you to match more complex and flexible patterns than simple fixed strings.

Regex is a vast topic in itself, but here are a few basic metacharacters commonly used with `grep`:

- **. (Dot):** Matches *any single character* (except newline). `c.t` would match "cat", "cot", "c_t", etc.
- *** (Asterisk):** Matches the *preceding* character or group zero or more times. `a*b` would match "b", "ab", "aab", "aaab", etc. `.*` matches any sequence of characters (or nothing).
- **^ (Caret):** Matches the beginning of a line. `^Start` matches lines that begin with "Start".
- **$ (Dollar sign):** Matches the end of a line. `end$` matches lines that end with "end".
- **[] (Square Brackets):** Matches any *one* character enclosed within the brackets. `[aeiou]` matches any lowercase vowel. `[0-9]` matches any digit. `[^0-9]` matches any character that is *not* a digit (when ^ is the first character inside []).

Let's try some basic regex:

```
# Find lines starting with 'root' in /etc/passwd
grep "^root" /etc/passwd

# Find lines ending with 'bash' in /etc/passwd
grep "bash$" /etc/passwd

# Find lines containing 'fail' or 'Fail'
grep "[Ff]ail" /var/log/auth.log # Might need sudo

# Find lines containing a sequence like 'tty' followed by any digit
grep "tty[0-9]" /var/log/auth.log # Might need sudo
```

By default, `grep` uses "Basic Regular Expressions" (BRE). For more advanced features (like + for one or more occurrences, ? for zero or one, | for alternation), you often need to use `egrep` (equivalent to `grep -E` for Extended Regular Expressions) or escape the special characters in BRE (e.g., \+, \|).

```
# Using egrep (or grep -E) to find lines with 'warn' or 'error' (case-
insensitive)
egrep -i "warn|error" /var/log/syslog # Might need sudo
```

Don't worry about mastering regex immediately. Start by using `grep` for simple text searches and gradually introduce basic patterns like ^, $, and [] as needed. It's a skill that develops over time.

Chapter Summary

This chapter equipped you with the essential tools for finding things on your Linux system. You learned the meticulous `find` command to search the live filesystem based on diverse criteria like name (-name, -iname), type (-type), size (-size), and time (-mtime), and how to execute actions (-exec, -delete) on the results. We contrasted this with the speedy `locate` command, which searches a pre-built database (updated by `updatedb`), ideal for quick filename lookups. Finally, and crucially, you learned how to search *inside* files for specific text patterns using `grep`, leveraging options like -i, -n, -v, -r, and getting a first taste of the power of regular expressions to define flexible search patterns.

Being able to find files and information efficiently is fundamental. Now that you're comfortable navigating, managing files, controlling processes, redirecting streams, and finding things, it's time to look more closely at the environment where all this happens: the shell itself. In the next chapter, we'll explore shell variables, aliases, history, and configuration files, learning how to customize your command-line environment to make it even more powerful and efficient.

Chapter 11: Understanding Your Shell

You've come a long way! You're navigating the filesystem, managing files and processes, redirecting data streams, and finding information like a seasoned pro. Throughout this journey, you've been interacting with Linux primarily through one crucial piece of software: the **shell**. We briefly introduced it back in Chapter 1 as your command interpreter, the translator between you and the kernel. Now, it's time to dive deeper into the shell itself, focusing on Bash (the Bourne Again SHell), which is the default on most Linux systems. Understanding how your shell works—how it manages variables, remembers your commands, lets you create shortcuts, and how you can configure it—will make your command-line experience significantly more efficient, personalized, and powerful. Let's peek behind the curtain of your command prompt.

What is a Shell Again? (Bash Focus)

As a quick refresher, the shell is a command-line interpreter. It's the program that presents you with a prompt (usually $), reads the commands you type, figures out what program needs to run to execute that command, asks the Linux kernel to run it, and then displays the output back to you.

While several shells exist (like zsh, fish, csh), **Bash** is the most common and widely used shell in the Linux world. It's an improved version of the original Bourne shell (sh) from the early days of UNIX. All the commands and techniques we've learned so far have been executed within Bash. Therefore, this chapter will focus specifically on Bash features and configuration.

Interactive vs. Non-Interactive Shells

It's helpful to understand that Bash can operate in different modes, primarily:

1. **Interactive Shell:** This is what you've been using. You get a prompt, type a command, press Enter, see the output, and get another prompt. You are *interacting* directly with the shell.
2. **Non-Interactive Shell:** This is typically when a shell runs a script (which we'll start exploring in Chapter 15). The shell reads commands from a file rather than directly from your keyboard, executes them, and usually doesn't display a prompt.

Why does this distinction matter? Because Bash often loads different configuration files depending on whether it's starting as an interactive login shell, an interactive non-login shell, or a non-interactive script-running shell. We'll see this when we discuss configuration files later in the chapter.

Shell Variables

Like variables in programming languages, shell variables are names that hold a value (usually a string of text). They are essential for storing temporary data, configuration settings, or information passed between commands. Bash uses two main types of variables: local shell variables and environment variables.

Local Shell Variables

A local shell variable exists only within the specific instance of the shell where it was created. It's not passed down to any programs or scripts that shell might start.

To create a local variable, you simply assign a value to a name using the = sign. **Crucially, there must be no spaces around the = sign.**

```
my_message="Hello from the shell!"
count=10
```

Variable names typically consist of letters, numbers, and underscores, usually starting with a letter or underscore. They are case-sensitive (count is different from Count).

To use the value stored in a variable, you prefix its name with a dollar sign ($):

```
echo $my_message
echo "The current count is: $count"

Hello from the shell!
The current count is: 10
```

If you start a *new* shell session (e.g., by typing `bash` and pressing Enter) and try to access $my_message, it won't be defined there. It was local to the original shell.

```
echo $my_message
# (Output is likely an empty line)
exit # Exit the new shell session
```

Environment Variables

Environment variables are special. They are not just local to the current shell; they are passed down to any **child processes** started by that shell. Think of them as settings or information that the shell makes available to all the programs it runs. This is how programs can learn about your username, your home directory location, or where to find other commands.

By convention, environment variable names are usually written in **UPPERCASE**.

Key Environment Variables

You've already encountered some important environment variables implicitly. Here are a few critical ones:

- PATH: This is arguably one of the most important. PATH contains a colon-separated list of directory paths. When you type a command (like `ls` or `grep`), the shell doesn't magically know where the executable file for that command is located. Instead, it searches through the directories listed in the PATH variable, in order, until it finds an executable file matching the command name. This is how `which` (from Chapter 5) finds commands.

  ```
  echo $PATH
  ```

  ```
  /usr/local/sbin:/usr/local/bin:/usr/sbin:/usr/bin:/sbin:/bin:/usr/
  games:/usr/local/games
  ```

  (Your PATH will likely look different.)

- HOME: Stores the absolute path to the current user's home directory. This is how commands like `cd` without arguments (or `cd ~`, see Chapter 2) know where to go.

  ```
  echo $HOME
  ```

```
/home/ada
```

- USER: Contains the username of the currently logged-in user. Used by various programs to identify you. (Similar to the output of `whoami` from Chapter 1).

  ```
  echo $USER

  ada
  ```

- SHELL: Specifies the path to the user's default login shell program.

  ```
  echo $SHELL

  /bin/bash
  ```

- PS1: This special variable defines the appearance of your primary shell prompt (the familiar $). We'll look at customizing this later in the chapter.

Viewing Environment Variables

Several commands let you see the environment variables currently set:

- env: Lists all environment variables and their values.
- printenv: Similar to env, but can also be used to print the value of a *specific* environment variable (e.g., `printenv HOME`).
- echo $VARNAME: As we've seen, you can always print a specific variable using echo.

```
# List all environment variables
env

# Print just the value of the TERM variable
printenv TERM

# Print the value of PS1
echo $PS1
```

Setting Environment Variables (`export`)

How do you create your own environment variable, or turn a local shell variable into an environment variable so that other programs you run can see it? You use the export command.

You can either define a local variable first and then export it:

```
# Create a local variable
MY_APP_CONFIG="/etc/my_app/production.conf"

# Make it an environment variable
export MY_APP_CONFIG

# Verify it's in the environment
env | grep MY_APP_CONFIG

MY_APP_CONFIG=/etc/my_app/production.conf
```

Or you can define and export it in a single step:

```
export EDITOR="nano"
export BROWSER="firefox"

# Verify
printenv EDITOR

nano
```

Now, if you run a program from this shell, it will inherit MY_APP_CONFIG, EDITOR, and BROWSER in its environment. Many programs look for specific environment variables to modify their behavior (e.g., many tools respect the EDITOR variable to determine which editor to use).

Remember: Changes made with export in the current shell only affect *that* shell session and its future child processes. They don't persist after you log out unless you add the export command to your shell configuration files.

Command History

Typing the same long commands repeatedly is tedious. Thankfully, Bash keeps a **history** of the commands you've recently executed, making it easy to recall and reuse them. Think of it like your web browser's history, but for the command line.

Viewing History

The `history` command displays a numbered list of commands from your history buffer:

```
history

 988  ls -l /etc
 989  cd ~/practice_files/
 990  grep -i "error" *.log
 991  sudo apt update
 992  sudo apt install htop
 993  htop
 994  man find
 995  find . -name "*.txt" -mtime -1
 996  history
```

(Your history will be completely different.)

Repeating Commands

Bash provides several shortcuts using the ! (bang) character to re-execute commands from history:

- !! **(bang bang)**: Executes the *very last* command again. This is extremely useful if you forgot to use sudo for a command that required it.

  ```
  apt install cowsay # Fails due to permissions
  # Output: E: Could not open lock file ... Permission denied
  sudo !! # Re-runs 'sudo apt install cowsay'
  ```

- !n: Executes command number n from the `history` list.

  ```
  # Rerun command 990 from the example above
  !990
  # Shell shows the command: grep -i "error" *.log
  # ... then executes it ...
  ```

- !string: Executes the most recent command in history that *starts* with string.

  ```
  # Rerun the most recent command starting with 'find'
  !find
  ```

```
# Shell shows: find . -name "*.txt" -mtime -1
# ... then executes it ...
```

Pitfall: Be careful with `!string`. If you type `!c` and the last command starting with c was `cat important_config > /dev/null` but you *meant* to run `cd ..`, you might get an unexpected result. It's often safer to use `Ctrl+R` for searching.

Searching History (`Ctrl+R`)

This is arguably the most efficient way to find and reuse commands. Pressing `Ctrl+R` initiates a **reverse-i-search** (reverse incremental search). As you start typing characters, Bash searches backward through your history and displays the most recent command matching the characters you've typed so far.

1. Press `Ctrl+R`. The prompt changes to `(reverse-i-search)`˙.
2. Start typing part of the command you want to find (e.g., `grep`).
3. The most recent command containing `grep` appears.
4. If it's the command you want, press `Enter` to execute it immediately, or press the `Right Arrow` or `End` key to place the command on the current prompt line for editing before execution.
5. If it's *not* the command you want, press `Ctrl+R` *again* to find the *next* older match containing the same characters.
6. If you want to cancel the search, press `Ctrl+G` or `Ctrl+C`.

Mastering `Ctrl+R` will save you an enormous amount of time and typing.

By default, Bash saves your command history in a file named `.bash_history` in your home directory when you exit a shell session.

Aliases: Creating Shortcuts

Do you find yourself frequently typing the same long command with specific options, like `ls -alh` or `grep -i --color=auto`? **Aliases** allow you to create short, custom names (shortcuts) for longer commands. Think of them like speed-dial numbers for your phone.

Defining Aliases

You define an alias using the `alias` command, followed by the desired alias name, an equals sign (=), and the command string enclosed in single quotes (').

```
# Create an alias 'll' for 'ls -alh'
alias ll='ls -alh'

# Create an alias 'update' to run system updates (Debian/Ubuntu example)
alias update='sudo apt update && sudo apt upgrade -y'

# Create an alias to show current network connections
alias ports='sudo netstat -tulnp'

# Create an alias to quickly clear the screen
alias cls='clear'
```

Now, instead of typing the full command, you can just type the alias name:

```
ll # Executes ls -alh
update # Executes sudo apt update && sudo apt upgrade -y
ports # Executes sudo netstat -tulnp
cls # Executes clear
```

Viewing and Removing Aliases

- To see all currently defined aliases, type `alias` with no arguments.
- To see the definition of a specific alias, type `alias name` (e.g., `alias ll`).
- To remove an alias for the current session, use `unalias name` (e.g., `unalias update`).

Making Aliases Permanent

Aliases defined directly in the shell like this only last for the current shell session. As soon as you log out or close the terminal, they are gone. To make your aliases available every time you start a shell, you need to add the `alias` definition lines to your shell's startup configuration file, typically `~/.bashrc`. We'll discuss this file next.

Shell Configuration Files

When Bash starts, it reads commands from various configuration files (also called startup files, dotfiles, or rc files) to set up your environment, define aliases and functions, set variables, and customize behavior. Understanding which files are read when is key to making persistent changes.

As mentioned earlier, the files read depend on whether the shell is a **login shell** or an **interactive non-login shell**.

- **Login Shell:** The first shell you get after logging in (e.g., via console, SSH, or sometimes the first terminal opened after graphical login).
- **Interactive Non-Login Shell:** A shell started *after* you've already logged in (e.g., opening a second terminal window in a GUI, typing bash in an existing shell).

Here's the typical loading sequence for user-specific files (system-wide files like /etc/profile and /etc/bashrc are also involved but less commonly modified by regular users):

1. **For Login Shells:** Bash looks for ~/.bash_profile, ~/.bash_login, and ~/.profile in that order. It reads and executes commands from the **first one it finds**. It does *not* read the others. Many systems default to creating ~/.profile for compatibility, or ~/.bash_profile.
2. **For Interactive Non-Login Shells:** Bash reads and executes commands from ~/.bashrc.

The .bashrc vs .bash_profile **Puzzle**

Wait, so if aliases are typically put in .bashrc, but login shells don't read .bashrc by default, how do aliases become available in login shells (like SSH sessions)?

The common solution is to add a few lines of code inside your ~/.bash_profile (or ~/.bash_login or ~/.profile) that explicitly tell it to *also* read the .bashrc file if it exists. This ensures settings defined in .bashrc are loaded for *both* types of interactive shells.

You'll often find code like this near the top of ~/.bash_profile or ~/.profile:

```
# if running bash
if [ -n "$BASH_VERSION" ]; then
    # include .bashrc if it exists
    if [ -f "$HOME/.bashrc" ]; then
        . "$HOME/.bashrc" # Note the '.' which means 'source'
    fi
fi
```

(This checks if the .bashrc file exists and, if so, executes the commands within it using the . or source command.)

Therefore, the generally recommended practice is:

- Put your **aliases, shell functions, prompt settings (PS1), and other interactive shell customizations** in ~/.bashrc.
- Put **environment variable settings (export VAR=value)** that should be set only once upon login (and inherited by all subsequent processes, including graphical ones sometimes) in ~/.bash_profile or ~/.profile.
- Ensure your ~/.bash_profile (or .profile) sources your ~/.bashrc using the pattern shown above.

Applying Changes

After you edit one of these configuration files (e.g., adding an alias to ~/.bashrc), the changes won't take effect in your *current* shell session automatically. You have two options:

1. **Start a New Shell:** Close your current terminal and open a new one. The new shell will read the updated configuration file.
2. **Source the File:** Use the source command (or its shorthand, a single dot .) to read and execute the commands from the file in your *current* shell.

```
# Apply changes made in .bashrc immediately
source ~/.bashrc
# Or equivalently:
. ~/.bashrc
```

Customizing Your Prompt (PS1)

Tired of the plain default prompt (like user@hostname:~$)? You can customize it! The appearance of your primary prompt is controlled by the PS1 environment variable. It contains a string with special escape sequences that Bash replaces with dynamic information.

First, see what your current PS1 looks like:

```
echo "$PS1"
```

(The output might look complex, possibly including color codes.)

Here are some common escape sequences you can use in PS1:

- \u: Username of the current user.
- \h: Hostname (up to the first dot).

- \H: Full hostname.
- \w: Current working directory (full path, with ~ for home).
- \W: Basename of the current working directory (~ for home).
- \$: Displays # if the effective UID is 0 (root), otherwise $.
- \n: A newline character.
- \d: Date in "Weekday Month Date" format (e.g., "Tue May 26").
- \t: Current time in 24-hour HH:MM:SS format.
- \@: Current time in 12-hour am/pm format.
- \!: History number of the current command.

Let's try creating a simple custom prompt: username@hostname:current_dir$

```
# Temporarily set PS1 for the current session
export PS1='\u@\h:\w\$ '
```

Your prompt should change immediately!

To make this prompt permanent, add that export PS1='...' line to your ~/.bashrc file and then run source ~/.bashrc.

Adding Color

You can make your prompt more visually appealing using ANSI escape codes for colors. The codes are enclosed within \[and \]. This tells Bash that the enclosed characters don't take up space on the line, which is important for correct line wrapping.

A common structure is \[\033[ColorCodeHere\]TextToColor\[\033[00m\]. \033[starts the code, m ends it, and \033[00m resets colors back to default.

Example color codes: 01;31m (bold red), 01;32m (bold green), 01;34m (bold blue), 00;36m (cyan).

Let's make the username green and the directory blue:

```
export PS1='\[\033[01;32m\]\u\[\033[00m\]@\h:\[\033[01;34m\]\w\[\033[00m\]\$ '
```

Color codes can make prompts look complex quickly, but they can also enhance readability. Experiment, but remember to add the final version to your .bashrc. Online "PS1 generators" can help you build complex prompts easily.

Chapter Summary

In this chapter, we delved into the workings of your command interpreter, the Bash shell. You learned the difference between interactive and non-interactive shells and explored the two types of variables: local shell variables and the crucial **environment variables** (like PATH, HOME, USER) which are inherited by child processes, viewed with env or printenv, and created with export. We mastered the command **history**, viewing it with history, re-executing commands with !!, !n, !string, and efficiently searching it with Ctrl+R. You discovered how to create time-saving **aliases** using alias and how to make them permanent. We navigated the important **shell configuration files**, understanding the roles of ~/.bash_profile (for login shells, often setting environment variables) and ~/.bashrc (for interactive non-login shells, ideal for aliases and functions), and the common practice of sourcing .bashrc from .bash_profile. Finally, you learned how to customize your prompt's appearance using the PS1 variable and its special escape sequences, even adding color.

By understanding and configuring your shell environment, you can create a more productive and personalized command-line workspace. Now that your environment is tuned, let's look at another practical task: bundling and compressing files for storage or transfer using tools like tar and gzip in the next chapter.

Chapter 12: Packing and Unpacking Files

You've become quite skilled at managing individual files and navigating your Linux system. But what happens when you need to bundle many files and directories together, perhaps to back them up, send them to someone else, or simply keep a project's files neatly contained? Or what if you need to make large files smaller to save disk space or reduce download times? This chapter introduces the standard Linux tools for **archiving** (bundling files together) and **compressing** (making files smaller). We'll focus on the classic `tar` command for archiving and combine it with common compression tools like `gzip`, `bzip2`, and `xz`. We'll also look at handling the familiar `.zip` format. Let's learn how to pack things up and shrink them down.

Archiving Files: `tar` (Tape Archive)

The `tar` command is the traditional UNIX and Linux utility for creating and manipulating archives, often called **tarballs**. Its name originates from Tape Archive, as it was initially designed to write sequential archives suitable for tape backups. While tapes are less common now, `tar` remains the standard way to bundle multiple files and directories into a single file, preserving permissions, ownership (if possible), and directory structures.

Think of `tar` like putting many items into a single cardboard box. The box itself groups everything together, making it easier to handle, but it doesn't necessarily make the contents smaller. The resulting file (the box) typically has a `.tar` extension.

`tar` has many options, but they usually revolve around three main modes of operation: creating (-c), extracting (-x), and listing (-t). Two other options are almost always used:

- -f FILE: Specifies the name of the archive file to operate on. This option *must* typically be followed immediately by the filename.
- -v: Operate verbosely, showing the names of the files being processed. This gives you feedback on what tar is doing.

Let's create a practice directory and some files (remember mkdir, touch, and echo from Chapter 3):

```
# Create a directory structure for our example
mkdir tar_practice
cd tar_practice
mkdir project_files
touch project_files/config.ini
echo "Report data..." > project_files/report.log
mkdir project_files/images
touch project_files/images/logo.png
touch notes.txt
echo "Final notes" >> notes.txt

# Verify our structure
ls -R project_files

project_files:
config.ini  images/  report.log

project_files/images:
logo.png
```

Creating Archives (-c)

To create a new archive, use the -c (create) option, along with -v (verbose) and -f (file). After -f, specify the desired archive filename (e.g., my_project.tar), followed by the files or directories you want to add to the archive.

```
# Create an archive named my_project.tar containing project_files and notes.txt
tar -cvf my_project.tar project_files/ notes.txt
```

The -v option will show you the files being added:

```
project_files/
project_files/config.ini
project_files/report.log
project_files/images/
```

```
project_files/images/logo.png
notes.txt
```

Now, if you list the current directory (`ls -l`), you'll see the `my_project.tar` file alongside the original files and directories.

```
ls -l

total 28
-rw-r--r-- 1 ada ada 10240 Jul 25 10:15 my_project.tar
-rw-r--r-- 1 ada ada    13 Jul 25 10:14 notes.txt
drwxr-xr-x 3 ada ada  4096 Jul 25 10:14 project_files
```

(Sizes and dates will vary)

Listing Archive Contents (-t)

Before extracting an archive (especially one you received from someone else), it's wise to check its contents without actually unpacking it. Use the -t (list, think **t**able of contents) option, along with -v (optional, but gives more detail) and -f.

```
# List the contents of my_project.tar
tar -tvf my_project.tar
```

This will show the paths, permissions, ownership, size, and modification times of the files stored *inside* the archive:

```
drwxr-xr-x ada/ada         0 2024-07-25 10:14 project_files/
-rw-r--r-- ada/ada         0 2024-07-25 10:14 project_files/config.ini
-rw-r--r-- ada/ada        15 2024-07-25 10:14 project_files/report.log
drwxr-xr-x ada/ada         0 2024-07-25 10:14 project_files/images/
-rw-r--r-- ada/ada         0 2024-07-25 10:14 project_files/images/logo.png
-rw-r--r-- ada/ada        13 2024-07-25 10:14 notes.txt
```

Extracting Archives (-x)

To extract the files from an archive back into the filesystem, use the -x (extract) option, typically with -v and -f.

```
# Let's make a new directory to extract into, to avoid overwriting
mkdir extraction_zone
```

```
cd extraction_zone

# Extract the contents of the archive (assuming it's one level up)
tar -xvf ../my_project.tar
```

The verbose output shows the files being extracted:

```
project_files/
project_files/config.ini
project_files/report.log
project_files/images/
project_files/images/logo.png
notes.txt
```

If you now `ls`, you'll see the `project_files` directory and `notes.txt` have been recreated inside `extraction_zone`.

```
ls -lR

.:
total 8
-rw-r--r-- 1 ada ada   13 Jul 25 10:14 notes.txt
drwxr-xr-x 3 ada ada 4096 Jul 25 10:14 project_files

./project_files:
total 4
-rw-r--r-- 1 ada ada    0 Jul 25 10:14 config.ini
drwxr-xr-x 2 ada ada 4096 Jul 25 10:14 images
-rw-r--r-- 1 ada ada   15 Jul 25 10:14 report.log

./project_files/images:
total 0
-rw-r--r-- 1 ada ada 0 Jul 25 10:14 logo.png
```

Important: By default, `tar` extracts files relative to the current directory. Be careful where you run `tar -xvf` from, especially if the archive contains absolute paths (which is rare and generally discouraged) or paths like `../`. It's often safest to create a dedicated directory and extract into it, as we did here. Also, `tar` will typically overwrite existing files with the same name without warning!

Compression Tools

tar bundles files, but it doesn't make them smaller. To save space or bandwidth, you need **compression**. Linux offers several excellent compression utilities. They typically work on a single file at a time, replacing the original file with a compressed version (adding a specific extension) or vice-versa during decompression.

gzip **and** gunzip **(.gz)**

gzip (GNU **zip**) is the most common and widely compatible compression tool on Linux. It offers a good balance between compression speed and size reduction. Files compressed with gzip usually have the .gz extension.

```
# Go back to the parent directory
cd ..

# Copy our tar file to experiment with
cp my_project.tar my_project_copy.tar

# Compress the copy using gzip
gzip my_project_copy.tar

# Check the result
ls -l my_project_copy.tar.gz
```

You'll see that my_project_copy.tar is gone, replaced by my_project_copy.tar.gz, which should be noticeably smaller.

```
-rw-r--r-- 1 ada ada  235 Jul 25 10:25 my_project_copy.tar.gz
```

(Size reduction depends on file content, but it's usually significant for text or tar archives.)

To decompress a .gz file, use gunzip (or gzip -d):

```
# Decompress the file
gunzip my_project_copy.tar.gz

# Check the result
ls -l my_project_copy.tar
```

The .gz file is gone, and the original .tar file is restored.

```
-rw-r--r-- 1 ada ada 10240 Jul 25 10:15 my_project_copy.tar
rm my_project_copy.tar # Clean up
```

bzip2 and bunzip2 (.bz2)

bzip2 generally offers **better compression** than gzip (meaning smaller file sizes) but is usually **slower** to compress and decompress. Files compressed with bzip2 have the .bz2 extension.

```
cp my_project.tar my_project_copy.tar

# Compress using bzip2
bzip2 my_project_copy.tar

ls -l my_project_copy.tar.bz2
```

The resulting .bz2 file might be even smaller than the .gz version.

```
-rw-r--r-- 1 ada ada  210 Jul 25 10:28 my_project_copy.tar.bz2
```

To decompress, use bunzip2 (or bzip2 -d):

```
bunzip2 my_project_copy.tar.bz2
ls -l my_project_copy.tar

-rw-r--r-- 1 ada ada 10240 Jul 25 10:15 my_project_copy.tar
rm my_project_copy.tar # Clean up
```

xz and unxz (.xz)

xz is a newer compression format that often achieves the **highest compression ratios** (smallest files), surpassing both gzip and bzip2. However, it tends to be the slowest, especially during compression. Files compressed with xz have the .xz extension.

```
cp my_project.tar my_project_copy.tar

# Compress using xz
xz my_project_copy.tar

ls -l my_project_copy.tar.xz
```

The `.xz` file is often the smallest of the three.

```
-rw-r--r-- 1 ada ada  195 Jul 25 10:30 my_project_copy.tar.xz
```

To decompress, use `unxz` (or `xz -d`):

```
unxz my_project_copy.tar.xz
ls -l my_project_copy.tar
```

```
-rw-r--r-- 1 ada ada 10240 Jul 25 10:15 my_project_copy.tar
rm my_project_copy.tar # Clean up
```

Which compression tool to choose?

- `gzip` (`.gz`): Best for compatibility and speed. Good default choice.
- `bzip2` (`.bz2`): Good when file size is more important than speed.
- `xz` (`.xz`): Best when smallest possible file size is critical, and you can tolerate slower compression/decompression times.

Combining Archiving and Compression with `tar`

Compressing a `.tar` file after creating it works, but it's a two-step process. Thankfully, the modern `tar` command can handle both archiving *and* compression/decompression simultaneously using specific options! This is the most common way compressed archives are created and handled on Linux.

The key options are:

- `-z`: Filter the archive through **gzip** (`.tar.gz` or `.tgz`)
- `-j`: Filter the archive through **bzip2** (`.tar.bz2` or `.tbz2`)
- `-J`: Filter the archive through **xz** (`.tar.xz` or `.txz`)

Creating Compressed Archives

You simply add the appropriate compression flag (`z`, `j`, or `J`) to your `-c` (create) command, and use the corresponding file extension for the output file.

```
# Create a gzipped tar archive
tar -czvf my_project.tar.gz project_files/ notes.txt

# Create a bzip2'd tar archive
tar -cjvf my_project.tar.bz2 project_files/ notes.txt
```

```
# Create an xz'd tar archive
tar -cJvf my_project.tar.xz project_files/ notes.txt

# Check the resulting file sizes
ls -l my_project.tar.*


-rw-r--r-- 1 ada ada  210 Jul 25 10:35 my_project.tar.bz2
-rw-r--r-- 1 ada ada  235 Jul 25 10:34 my_project.tar.gz
-rw-r--r-- 1 ada ada  195 Jul 25 10:36 my_project.tar.xz
```

(These files contain the same content as `my_project.tar` *but are compressed.)*

Extracting Compressed Archives

The beauty is that for extraction (-x), you often **don't even need to specify the compression flag**. Modern `tar` usually auto-detects the compression type based on the file extension and applies the correct filter.

```
# Go back to our extraction zone (and clean it first)
cd extraction_zone
rm -rf project_files/ notes.txt

# Extract the .tar.gz archive (no -z needed, usually)
tar -xvf ../my_project.tar.gz
ls # Should see project_files and notes.txt

rm -rf project_files/ notes.txt # Clean again

# Extract the .tar.bz2 archive (no -j needed, usually)
tar -xvf ../my_project.tar.bz2
ls

rm -rf project_files/ notes.txt # Clean again

# Extract the .tar.xz archive (no -J needed, usually)
tar -xvf ../my_project.tar.xz
ls
```

In each case, `tar` should successfully decompress and extract the contents. While auto-detection is convenient, explicitly providing the correct flag (-z, -j, or -J) along with -xvf can sometimes be necessary if the filename extension is missing or unusual, or if you're using a very old version of `tar`.

Listing Compressed Archives

Similarly, you can use -t to list the contents of compressed archives, usually without needing the compression flag:

```
tar -tvf ../my_project.tar.gz
tar -tvf ../my_project.tar.bz2
tar -tvf ../my_project.tar.xz
```

Each command will list the contents stored within the respective compressed archive.

Working with Zip Files: `zip` **and** `unzip`

While `tar` combined with `gzip/bzip2/xz` is the standard in the Linux/UNIX world, you will inevitably encounter .zip files, which are the standard archive format in the Windows world. Linux provides the `zip` and `unzip` commands to handle these. They might not be installed by default, but are easily added using your package manager (Chapter 13):

```
# Debian/Ubuntu
sudo apt update && sudo apt install zip unzip

# Fedora/CentOS/RHEL
sudo dnf install zip unzip
```

Creating Zip Archives

The basic syntax for `zip` is `zip archive_name.zip file1 file2 directory1 ...`. To include the contents of directories recursively, use the -r option.

```
# Go back to the parent tar_practice directory
cd ..

# Create a zip archive containing project_files and notes.txt
zip -r my_project.zip project_files/ notes.txt
```

`zip` will show the files being added and potentially the compression achieved:

```
  adding: project_files/ (stored 0%)
  adding: project_files/config.ini (stored 0%)
  adding: project_files/report.log (deflated 15%)
  adding: project_files/images/ (stored 0%)
```

```
  adding: project_files/images/logo.png (stored 0%)
  adding: notes.txt (stored 0%)
```

Extracting Zip Archives

To extract files from a .zip archive, use the unzip command:

```
# Go back to our extraction zone (and clean it first)
cd extraction_zone
rm -rf project_files/ notes.txt

# Extract the zip file
unzip ../my_project.zip
```

unzip will list the files as it extracts them:

```
Archive:  ../my_project.zip
   creating: project_files/
 extracting: project_files/config.ini
 extracting: project_files/report.log
   creating: project_files/images/
 extracting: project_files/images/logo.png
 extracting: notes.txt
```

Like tar, unzip extracts relative to the current directory and will often prompt you if a file already exists, asking if you want to overwrite it. You can use unzip -l my_project.zip to list the contents without extracting.

While zip and unzip are essential for cross-platform compatibility, tar combined with gzip/bzip2/xz is generally preferred within Linux environments as it handles Linux permissions and file types more robustly.

Chapter Summary

In this chapter, you learned the vital skills of bundling and compressing files. We differentiated between **archiving** (grouping files with tar) and **compressing** (shrinking files with tools like gzip, bzip2, xz). You mastered the core tar operations: creating archives (tar -cvf), listing their contents (tar -tvf), and extracting them (tar -xvf). We explored the common compression utilities and their trade-offs regarding speed versus compression ratio. Most importantly, you learned how to combine archiving and compression seamlessly using tar options (-z, -j, -J) to create and extract standard Linux compressed archives like `.tar.gz`, `.tar.bz2`, and `.tar.xz`. Finally, we covered how to handle `.zip` files using the `zip` and `unzip` commands for cross-platform compatibility.

You can now efficiently package and shrink files for backup, distribution, or storage. With files managed, processes controlled, and archives handled, a major remaining area is managing the software *itself* on your system. In the next chapter, we'll explore Linux package managers like `apt` and `dnf`, which allow you to easily install, update, and remove software applications and libraries.

Chapter 13: Managing Software

You've journeyed through the filesystem, tamed running processes, and learned to bundle files with `tar` and compression tools (Chapter 12). Your Linux command-line skills are growing! But what about adding *new* capabilities to your system? How do you install that cool text editor someone recommended, the web server you want to experiment with, or the programming language you need for a project? Unlike some other operating systems where you might download an installer from a website and click through wizards, Linux distributions typically use a much more streamlined, powerful, and centralized approach called **package management**. This chapter demystifies how software is typically distributed and installed on Linux and introduces you to the essential package manager commands for Debian/Ubuntu (`apt`) and Fedora/RHEL (`dnf`) systems.

How Linux Software is Distributed

Before diving into the tools, let's understand the forms software can take and where it comes from in the Linux world.

Source Code vs. Pre-compiled Binaries

Software fundamentally starts as human-readable **source code**, written in programming languages like C, Python, or Java. To actually run this code, it usually needs to be translated into machine-understandable instructions called **binary** code (or interpreted by another program like the Python interpreter).

- **Source Code Distribution:** Because Linux and its ecosystem are heavily based on open source, you can almost always get the original source code for applications. You could theoretically download this source code, install the necessary development tools (compilers, libraries), configure it for your specific system, compile it into binary code, and then install it manually.

- **Pre-compiled Binaries:** While compiling from source offers ultimate flexibility, it can be complex, time-consuming, and requires managing dependencies (more on that soon!) manually. For most users, a much more convenient approach is to use **pre-compiled binaries**. These are versions of the software that have already been compiled by the distribution maintainers for your specific system architecture (like x86_64). They are packaged up, ready to be installed and run.

Package managers almost exclusively deal with pre-compiled binary packages.

Repositories: Your Software Warehouse

So, where do these pre-compiled packages live? They reside in **repositories** (often called "repos"). A repository is essentially a large, centralized server (or network of servers) that stores collections of software packages specifically built and tested for a particular Linux distribution and version.

Think of a repository like a massive, well-organized warehouse or an app store. Your distribution knows the address of its official warehouses. When you ask to install a piece of software, your system contacts the repository, finds the right package, downloads it, and installs it.

Major distributions maintain official repositories containing thousands of packages, ensuring they work correctly with the rest of the system and receive security updates. There are also third-party repositories for software not included in the official ones, but adding them requires careful consideration of trust and potential conflicts.

Introduction to Package Managers

This brings us to the **package manager**. It's the command-line tool that acts as your interface to the repository system. It's the forklift driver and inventory manager for your software warehouse.

The Role of a Package Manager

A package manager automates the process of:

1. **Installing:** Finding the requested software in the repositories, downloading the correct package files, and placing them in the appropriate locations on your filesystem.

2. **Updating:** Checking the repositories for newer versions of your installed software and upgrading them, often including security patches.
3. **Removing:** Deleting software packages and their associated files cleanly from your system.
4. **Querying:** Searching for available packages, viewing information about installed or available packages, and listing installed packages.

Handling Dependencies: The Magic Ingredient

Perhaps the *most* critical job of a package manager is **dependency management**. Modern software is rarely self-contained. A graphical application might need specific graphics libraries, a web server might need encryption libraries, and a development tool might need a specific compiler version. These required external components are called **dependencies**.

Imagine trying to build a complex model car. You need the main body, but also wheels, axles, glue, paint, specific screws, etc. If you had to find each tiny screw and the right type of glue yourself from different stores, it would be incredibly frustrating.

Manually installing software and tracking its dependencies is similarly painful. You might install program A, only to find it needs library B. You install library B, but it needs library C version 2.0 or higher. You install library C, but that conflicts with another program that needs version 1.5! This nightmare is often called "dependency hell."

Package managers solve this beautifully. When you ask to install a package (say, `cool-app`), the package manager checks its dependency list. It sees that `cool-app` requires `library-x` and `utility-y`. It then checks if you already have compatible versions installed. If not, it automatically downloads and installs `library-x` and `utility-y` *before* installing `cool-app`. It resolves the entire chain of requirements, ensuring everything needed is present and compatible (within the confines of the repository's offerings). This automated dependency resolution is a cornerstone of Linux usability.

Debian-Based Systems (Ubuntu, Debian): `apt`

Distributions derived from Debian (including Ubuntu, Linux Mint, Pop!_OS, and many others) use the **Debian Package management system**. The underlying tool that handles individual package files (`.deb` files) is `dpkg`. However, the much more user-friendly command-line interface you'll typically use is `apt` (Advanced Packaging Tool). (You might also see the older `apt-get` command in older tutorials; `apt` is generally preferred now as it combines functionalities and has a nicer progress bar).

Most apt commands that modify the system (install, remove, upgrade) require administrator privileges, so you'll usually prefix them with sudo (from Chapter 7).

Updating Package Lists (sudo apt update)

Before installing or upgrading, you **must** tell apt to refresh its list of available packages from the repositories configured on your system. This ensures you're seeing the latest available versions and dependencies. Think of it as getting the latest catalog from the warehouse.

```
sudo apt update
```

This command doesn't upgrade any software; it just downloads the latest package information (like lists of package names, versions, and dependencies).

```
Hit:1 http://gb.archive.ubuntu.com/ubuntu jammy InRelease
Get:2 http://gb.archive.ubuntu.com/ubuntu jammy-updates InRelease [119 kB]
Get:3 http://security.ubuntu.com/ubuntu jammy-security InRelease [114 kB]
... Fetched 1,500 kB in 2s (750 kB/s)
Reading package lists... Done
Building dependency tree... Done
Reading state information... Done
All packages are up to date.
```

Upgrading Packages (sudo apt upgrade)

Once you've updated the package lists, you can upgrade all installed packages to their newest available versions (as listed in the refreshed catalog):

```
sudo apt upgrade
```

apt will show you which packages are going to be upgraded and how much data needs to be downloaded. It will usually ask for confirmation (Y/n) before proceeding.

```
Reading package lists... Done
Building dependency tree... Done
Reading state information... Done
Calculating upgrade... Done
The following packages will be upgraded:
   firefox libavcodec58 libavutil56 ... (many packages) ...
25 upgraded, 0 newly installed, 0 to remove and 0 not upgraded.
Need to get 150 MB of archives.
```

```
After this operation, 10.5 MB of additional disk space will be used.
Do you want to continue? [Y/n] y
Get:1 http://gb.archive.ubuntu.com/ubuntu jammy-updates/main amd64 firefox amd64
128.0.1+build1-0ubuntu0.22.04.1 [75.8 MB]
... (downloads packages) ...
Setting up firefox (128.0.1+build1-0ubuntu0.22.04.1) ...
... (configures packages) ...
```

Note: Sometimes, upgrading packages might require removing other packages or installing new ones due to complex dependency changes. In these cases, `apt upgrade` might hold back those upgrades. The command `sudo apt full-upgrade` (or the older `dist-upgrade`) handles these situations more aggressively, potentially removing packages if needed to complete the upgrade. Use `full-upgrade` with a bit more caution, ensuring you review the proposed changes.

Searching for Packages (`apt search`)

Don't know the exact name of the package you want? Use `apt search` followed by keywords.

```
# Search for packages related to the 'htop' process viewer
apt search htop

Sorting... Done
Full Text Search... Done
htop/jammy 3.0.5-7build2 amd64
  interactive processes viewer

atop/jammy 2.7.1-1 amd64
  Monitor for system resources and process activity
... (other related packages) ...
```

Viewing Package Information (`apt show`)

Once you have a potential package name, you can get more details about it using `apt show`.

```
apt show htop

Package: htop
Version: 3.0.5-7build2
Priority: optional
```

```
Section: utils
Origin: Ubuntu
Maintainer: Ubuntu Developers <ubuntu-devel-discuss@lists.ubuntu.com>
...
Depends: libc6 (>= 2.34), libncursesw6 (>= 6), libtinfo6 (>= 6)
Homepage: https://htop.dev/
Description: interactive processes viewer
 Htop is an interactive text-mode process viewer for Unix systems.
 It aims to be a better 'top'.
 ...
```

This shows the version, dependencies, description, and other useful metadata.

Installing Packages (sudo apt install)

This is the core command for adding new software.

```
# Install the 'htop' package
sudo apt install htop
```

apt will calculate dependencies, tell you which additional packages (if any) need to be installed, confirm the disk space required, and ask for confirmation.

```
Reading package lists... Done
Building dependency tree... Done
Reading state information... Done
The following NEW packages will be installed:
  htop
0 upgraded, 1 newly installed, 0 to remove and 0 not upgraded.
Need to get 90.1 kB of archives.
After this operation, 261 kB of additional disk space will be used.
Do you want to continue? [Y/n] y
Get:1 http://gb.archive.ubuntu.com/ubuntu jammy/main amd64 htop amd64 3.0.5-
7build2 [90.1 kB]
Fetched 90.1 kB in 0s (500 kB/s)
Selecting previously unselected package htop.
(Reading database ... 150000 files and directories currently installed.)
Preparing to unpack .../htop_3.0.5-7build2_amd64.deb ...
Unpacking htop (3.0.5-7build2) ...
Setting up htop (3.0.5-7build2) ...
Processing triggers for man-db (2.10.2-1) ...
```

Now you can run the htop command!

Removing Packages (`sudo apt remove`, `sudo apt purge`)

To uninstall software, use `apt remove`.

```
sudo apt remove htop
```

This removes the package files but often leaves behind user configuration files (in case you want to reinstall later and keep your settings).

```
Reading package lists... Done
Building dependency tree... Done
Reading state information... Done
The following packages will be REMOVED:
  htop
0 upgraded, 0 newly installed, 1 to remove and 0 not upgraded.
After this operation, 261 kB disk space will be freed.
Do you want to continue? [Y/n] y
(Reading database ... 150095 files and directories currently installed.)
Removing htop (3.0.5-7build2) ...
Processing triggers for man-db (2.10.2-1) ...
```

If you want to remove the package *and* its system-wide configuration files, use `apt purge`:

```
sudo apt purge htop
```

(The output looks similar to `remove`, but configuration files are also deleted).

apt also often suggests running `sudo apt autoremove` after removing packages. This command removes dependencies that were installed automatically for removed packages and are no longer needed by any other installed software, helping to keep your system clean.

Red Hat-Based Systems (Fedora, CentOS, RHEL): dnf / yum

Distributions in the Red Hat family (Fedora, CentOS Stream, Red Hat Enterprise Linux, AlmaLinux, Rocky Linux, etc.) use the **RPM** (originally Red Hat Package Manager) package format (`.rpm` files).

For many years, the primary command-line tool was yum (Yellowdog Updater, Modified). However, yum had some limitations, particularly in dependency resolution performance. Its successor is dnf (**Dan**dified **YUM**), which provides better performance, more predictable behavior, and a cleaner codebase while largely maintaining compatibility with yum commands. On modern Fedora, RHEL 8+, and CentOS 8+, dnf is the standard tool. You might still encounter yum on older systems (like CentOS 7). We will focus on dnf, but most commands work identically if you substitute yum for dnf.

Like apt, dnf commands that change the system typically require sudo.

Checking for Updates (`sudo dnf check-update`)

Similar to apt update, but dnf check-update only *lists* available updates without refreshing the cache quite as explicitly (though it often does implicitly). It tells you what *would* be upgraded.

```
sudo dnf check-update

Fedora 39 - x86_64 - Updates                 7.5 MB/s |  22 MB     00:02
Security checking servers.
Obsoleting Packages
libavdevice.i686                    5.1.4-1.fc39      updates-testing
  libavdevice-free.i686             6.0.1-3.fc39      fedora

Packages marked obsoleting not shown.

firefox.x86_64                          128.0.1-1.fc39      updates
kernel.x86_64                           6.9.6-200.fc39      updates
kernel-core.x86_64                      6.9.6-200.fc39      updates
...
```

Upgrading Packages (`sudo dnf upgrade`)

To actually perform the upgrade of all packages, use dnf upgrade:

```
sudo dnf upgrade
```

dnf will resolve dependencies, show you the list of packages to be upgraded, installed, or removed, and ask for confirmation.

```
Last metadata expiration check: 0:00:15 ago on Thu 25 Jul 2024 11:15:30 BST.
Dependencies resolved.
================================================================================
 Package          Architecture    Version               Repository       Size
================================================================================
```

```
Upgrading:
 firefox        x86_64          128.0.1-1.fc39          updates        105 M
 kernel         x86_64          6.9.6-200.fc39          updates        165 k
 kernel-core    x86_64          6.9.6-200.fc39          updates         52 M
 ...

Transaction Summary
================================================================================
Upgrade  20 Packages

Total download size: 250 M
Is this ok [y/N]: y
Downloading Packages:
(1/20): kernel-6.9.6-200.fc39.x86_64.rpm         1.5 MB/s | 165 kB      00:00
...
Running transaction check
Transaction check succeeded.
Running transaction test
Transaction test succeeded.
Running transaction
  Preparing        :                                                    1/1
  Upgrading        : kernel-core-6.9.6-200.fc39.x86_64                   1/40
  Upgrading        : kernel-modules-6.9.6-200.fc39.x86_64                2/40
...
  Cleanup          : kernel-core-6.9.5-200.fc39.x86_64                  39/40
  Cleanup          : kernel-modules-6.9.5-200.fc39.x86_64               40/40
  Running scriptlet: kernel-core-6.9.5-200.fc39.x86_64                  40/40
  Verifying        : firefox-128.0.1-1.fc39.x86_64                       1/40
...

Upgraded:
  firefox-128.0.1-1.fc39.x86_64            kernel-6.9.6-200.fc39.x86_64 ...

Complete!
```

Searching for Packages (dnf search)

Use dnf search to find packages matching keywords.

```
dnf search htop

Last metadata expiration check: 0:15:10 ago on Thu 25 Jul 2024 11:15:30 BST.
========================= Name Exactly Matched: htop =========================
htop.x86_64 : Interactive process viewer
======================= Name & Summary Matched: htop ========================
pcp-gui.x86_64 : Performance Co-Pilot (PCP) graphical tools
```

Viewing Package Information (`dnf info`)

To get detailed information about a package:

```
dnf info htop

Last metadata expiration check: 0:16:20 ago on Thu 25 Jul 2024 11:15:30 BST.
Available Packages
Name         : htop
Version      : 3.3.0
Release      : 1.fc39
Architecture : x86_64
Size         : 131 k
Source       : htop-3.3.0-1.fc39.src.rpm
Repository   : fedora
Summary      : Interactive process viewer
URL          : https://htop.dev/
License      : GPLv2+
Description  : htop is an interactive process viewer for Linux.
             : It aims to be a better top(1).
```

Installing Packages (`sudo dnf install`)

Use `dnf install` to add new software.

```
sudo dnf install htop
```

dnf resolves dependencies and asks for confirmation:

```
Last metadata expiration check: 0:17:05 ago on Thu 25 Jul 2024 11:15:30 BST.
Dependencies resolved.
================================================================================
 Package        Architecture      Version            Repository          Size
================================================================================
Installing:
 htop           x86_64            3.3.0-1.fc39        fedora             131 k

Transaction Summary
================================================================================
Install  1 Package

Total download size: 131 k
Installed size: 305 k
Is this ok [y/N]: y
Downloading Packages:
```

```
htop-3.3.0-1.fc39.x86_64.rpm                      1.1 MB/s | 131 kB      00:00
--------------------------------------------------------------------------------
Total                                             650 kB/s | 131 kB      00:00
Running transaction check
Transaction check succeeded.
Running transaction test
Transaction test succeeded.
Running transaction
  Preparing        :                                                      1/1
  Installing       : htop-3.3.0-1.fc39.x86_64                             1/1
  Running scriptlet: htop-3.3.0-1.fc39.x86_64                             1/1
  Verifying        : htop-3.3.0-1.fc39.x86_64                             1/1

Installed:
  htop-3.3.0-1.fc39.x86_64

Complete!
```

Removing Packages (sudo dnf remove)

To uninstall a package:

```
sudo dnf remove htop

Dependencies resolved.
================================================================================
 Package        Architecture      Version           Repository          Size
================================================================================
Removing:
 htop           x86_64            3.3.0-1.fc39      @fedora             305 k

Transaction Summary
================================================================================
Remove   1 Package

Freed space: 305 k
Is this ok [y/N]: y
Running transaction check
Transaction check succeeded.
Running transaction test
Transaction test succeeded.
Running transaction
  Preparing        :                                                      1/1
  Erasing          : htop-3.3.0-1.fc39.x86_64                             1/1
  Verifying        : htop-3.3.0-1.fc39.x86_64                             1/1
```

```
Removed:
  htop-3.3.0-1.fc39.x86_64

Complete!
```

Like apt, dnf also has an autoremove command (sudo dnf autoremove) to clean up unused dependencies. dnf remove typically removes configuration files as well, behaving more like apt purge by default in that regard.

Choosing the Right Package

Sometimes, searching reveals multiple packages with similar names. How do you choose?

- **Read Descriptions:** Use apt show or dnf info to carefully read the package descriptions.
- **Check for -dev/-devel:** If you are a developer and need header files or libraries to compile software *against* a package, you often need to install the corresponding development package. These typically end in -dev (Debian/Ubuntu) or -devel (Fedora/RHEL). For example, to compile code using the libcurl library, you might need libcurl4-openssl-dev or libcurl-devel. Regular users usually don't need these packages.
- **Consider Stability:** Different distributions (and different repositories within them) prioritize stability versus having the absolute latest software versions. For critical systems, relying on the stable, well-tested versions from the official repositories is usually best. For cutting-edge features, you might look at testing repositories or specific third-party sources (with caution).
- **Look at Dependencies:** Sometimes, examining the dependencies listed by apt show or dnf info can give clues about a package's purpose or scope.

When in doubt, using the main package name without extra suffixes (like -dev) is usually what you want for simply *using* an application.

Chapter Summary

This chapter peeled back the layers on how software installation works in the Linux ecosystem. You learned about source code versus pre-compiled binaries and the crucial role of **repositories** as centralized software sources. We introduced **package managers** as the essential tools that automate installing, updating, removing, and querying software, highlighting their ability to handle complex **dependencies** automatically.

We then covered the specific commands for the two major package management families: `apt` (for Debian/Ubuntu systems) with commands like `update`, `upgrade`, `install`, `remove`, `purge`, `search`, and `show`; and `dnf` (for Fedora/RHEL systems) with its similar commands `upgrade`, `install`, `remove`, `search`, and `info`. Finally, we touched upon tips for choosing the correct package when multiple options exist.

You're now empowered to install and manage software on your Linux system efficiently and reliably, leveraging the strengths of package management. Software often needs to communicate with other systems or access resources online. In the next chapter, we'll equip you with basic command-line tools for exploring network configurations and testing connectivity.

Chapter 14: Basic Networking Commands

Up to this point, our journey has largely focused on managing your own Linux system – the files, processes, software, and shell environment within its boundaries. But modern computing is rarely isolated; systems constantly communicate across networks, whether it's the local network in your home or office, or the vast expanse of the internet. Understanding the basics of network configuration and being able to perform simple diagnostics from the command line is an essential skill. This chapter introduces fundamental networking commands that let you check your system's network identity, test connectivity, resolve names, download files from the web, and securely connect to other machines. Let's plug into the network!

Checking Network Interfaces and IP Addresses

How does your computer identify itself on a network? Just like your house needs a unique postal address to receive mail, your computer needs a unique network address to send and receive data. The most common addressing scheme today is the **Internet Protocol (IP)**. You'll primarily encounter **IPv4** addresses (like `192.168.1.100` or `10.0.0.5`) and increasingly **IPv6** addresses (longer hexadecimal numbers like `2001:0db8:85a3:0000:0000:8a2e:0370:7334`).

Each network connection point on your computer (like a wired Ethernet port or a Wi-Fi adapter) is called a **network interface**. Each active interface usually gets assigned at least one IP address.

The Modern Approach: `ip addr`

The modern command for displaying information about your network interfaces and their addresses is `ip addr` (part of the versatile `ip` command suite).

```
ip addr show
# You can often omit 'show'
# ip addr
```

The output can look a bit dense at first, listing all network interfaces, including the special **loopback** interface (lo).

```
1: lo: <LOOPBACK,UP,LOWER_UP> mtu 65536 qdisc noqueue state UNKNOWN group
default qlen 1000
    link/loopback 00:00:00:00:00:00 brd 00:00:00:00:00:00
    inet 127.0.0.1/8 scope host lo
       valid_lft forever preferred_lft forever
    inet6 ::1/128 scope host
       valid_lft forever preferred_lft forever
2: eth0: <BROADCAST,MULTICAST,UP,LOWER_UP> mtu 1500 qdisc fq_codel state UP
group default qlen 1000
    link/ether 08:00:27:a1:b2:c3 brd ff:ff:ff:ff:ff:ff
    inet 192.168.1.105/24 brd 192.168.1.255 scope global dynamic noprefixroute
eth0
       valid_lft 85678sec preferred_lft 85678sec
    inet6 fe80::a00:27ff:fea1:b2c3/64 scope link noprefixroute
       valid_lft forever preferred_lft forever
3: wlan0: <BROADCAST,MULTICAST,UP,LOWER_UP> mtu 1500 qdisc noqueue state UP
group default qlen 1000
    link/ether 1c:b7:2c:d1:e2:f4 brd ff:ff:ff:ff:ff:ff
    inet 10.0.1.50/24 brd 10.0.1.255 scope global dynamic noprefixroute wlan0
       valid_lft 3450sec preferred_lft 3450sec
    inet6 fe80::1eb7:2cff:fed1:e2f4/64 scope link
       valid_lft forever preferred_lft forever
```

(Output varies greatly depending on your system and network configuration)

Let's break down the key parts for a typical interface like eth0 (often a wired Ethernet card) or wlan0 (a wireless card):

- 2: eth0:: The interface index (2) and name (eth0). Names can vary (enpXsY, ensX, etc.).
- <...UP...>: Flags indicating the interface status. UP means the interface is active.
- mtu 1500: Maximum Transmission Unit (packet size in bytes).
- link/ether 08:00:27:a1:b2:c3: The hardware **MAC address** (Media Access Control address), a unique identifier burned into the network card by the manufacturer.

- `inet 192.168.1.105/24`: The **IPv4 address** (192.168.1.105) and its **subnet mask** (/24, which corresponds to 255.255.255.0). The subnet mask defines which part of the address identifies the local network and which part identifies the specific host.
- `inet6 fe80::.../64`: An IPv6 address (this example is a link-local address).
- `scope global / scope link`: Indicates the reachability of the address (global means internet-routable, link means only on the local network segment).

The `lo` (loopback) interface with address `127.0.0.1` is a special virtual interface that allows the computer to talk to itself, often used for testing network services running locally.

The Older Command: `ifconfig`

You might see the `ifconfig` command mentioned in older guides or used on older systems. It serves a similar purpose to `ip addr`.

```
# May require installation or be in /sbin
# sudo apt install net-tools OR sudo dnf install net-tools
ifconfig
```

Its output format is different but provides much of the same information (IP address - `inet addr`, MAC address - `HWaddr`, interface status - `UP`). While `ifconfig` can still be used, the `ip` command (`ip addr`, `ip link`, `ip route`) is the modern standard and offers more functionality. It's recommended to get comfortable with `ip addr`.

Testing Network Connectivity: `ping`

How do you check if your computer can reach another computer on the network or the internet? The `ping` command is your basic connectivity tester. It sends a special network packet (an ICMP "echo request") to a target host, and if the host is reachable and configured to respond, it sends back an "echo reply".

Think of it like shouting "Marco!" across a pool. If you hear "Polo!" back, you know someone is there and can hear you.

The basic usage is simple:

```
ping hostname_or_IP
```

Let's try pinging a well-known public server, like one of Google's DNS servers (8.8.8.8), or a hostname like google.com:

```
ping 8.8.8.8
# Or: ping google.com
```

ping will run continuously, sending one packet per second (by default) and printing a line for each reply received:

```
PING 8.8.8.8 (8.8.8.8) 56(84) bytes of data.
64 bytes from 8.8.8.8: icmp_seq=1 ttl=116 time=15.2 ms
64 bytes from 8.8.8.8: icmp_seq=2 ttl=116 time=14.8 ms
64 bytes from 8.8.8.8: icmp_seq=3 ttl=116 time=15.5 ms
64 bytes from 8.8.8.8: icmp_seq=4 ttl=116 time=14.9 ms
^C
--- 8.8.8.8 ping statistics ---
4 packets transmitted, 4 received, 0% packet loss, time 3005ms
rtt min/avg/max/mdev = 14.800/15.100/15.500/0.270 ms
```

To stop ping, you need to press Ctrl+C.

Key parts of the output:

- `64 bytes from 8.8.8.8`: A reply was received from the target IP.
- `icmp_seq=1`: The sequence number of the packet (helps detect lost packets).
- `ttl=116`: Time To Live. A counter that decreases as the packet travels across routers; helps prevent packets from looping forever.
- `time=15.2 ms`: Round-Trip Time (RTT). How long it took for the request to go out and the reply to come back, in milliseconds. This is a basic measure of network latency. Lower is generally better.
- **Summary (after Ctrl+C):** Shows how many packets were sent and received, the percentage of packet loss, and statistics on the round-trip times.

Common Uses:

- Checking if your computer has basic internet connectivity.
- Checking if a specific server or device on your local network is online and responding.
- Getting a rough idea of network latency to a host.

Pitfalls:

- Many firewalls are configured to **block incoming ping requests** for security reasons. Just because a host doesn't reply to ping doesn't *absolutely* guarantee it's offline; it might just be ignoring you.
- `ping` only tests basic reachability; it doesn't tell you if a specific service (like a web server) is running on the target host.

You can use the `-c count` option to send only a specific number of pings and then stop automatically:

```
# Send only 3 pings
ping -c 3 google.com
```

Checking Network Routes: `ip route`

When your computer sends data to an IP address outside its immediate local network, how does it know where to send it *first*? It consults its **routing table**. The routing table contains rules that tell the system which network interface to use and which router (or **gateway**) address to forward the data to, based on the destination IP address.

Think of it like looking at road signs or asking for directions at an intersection. You don't need to know the *entire* path to your final destination instantly, just the next step or the main highway to get onto.

The command to view the main routing table is `ip route show` (or often just `ip route`):

```
ip route

default via 192.168.1.1 dev eth0 proto dhcp metric 100
10.0.1.0/24 dev wlan0 proto kernel scope link src 10.0.1.50 metric 600
192.168.1.0/24 dev eth0 proto kernel scope link src 192.168.1.105 metric 100
```

(Output depends heavily on your network setup)

The most important line for general internet connectivity is usually the `default` **route**:

- `default via 192.168.1.1`: This means for any destination address that doesn't match a more specific rule in the table, send the traffic to the gateway router located at IP address `192.168.1.1`.
- `dev eth0`: Send the traffic out using the `eth0` network interface.

- `proto dhcp`: Indicates this route was likely learned automatically via DHCP (Dynamic Host Configuration Protocol).
- `metric 100`: A preference value (lower is generally more preferred if multiple routes exist).

The other lines usually define routes for the directly connected local networks (e.g., `192.168.1.0/24` is reachable directly via `eth0`).

Looking at the default route is often helpful when troubleshooting general internet connection problems – it tells you which device acts as your gateway. The older command `route -n` provides similar information in a different format.

Querying DNS: `host`, `dig`, `nslookup`

Computers communicate using numerical IP addresses, but humans find it much easier to remember names like `www.google.com` or `wikipedia.org`. The **Domain Name System (DNS)** is the internet's distributed directory service that translates these human-friendly domain names into computer-friendly IP addresses.

When you type a name into your browser or use a hostname with `ping` or `ssh`, your system performs a DNS query (usually by asking a configured DNS server, often provided by your ISP or network administrator) to find the corresponding IP address. Sometimes, you need to perform these lookups manually for troubleshooting or information gathering.

Simple Lookup: `host`

The `host` command is a straightforward tool for simple DNS lookups.

```
host google.com

google.com has address 142.250.179.142
google.com has IPv6 address 2a00:1450:4009:824::200e
google.com mail is handled by 10 smtp.google.com.
```

This shows the IPv4 (`address`) and IPv6 addresses associated with `google.com`. It also shows the Mail Exchanger (`mail is handled by`) records, indicating which server handles email for that domain.

Detailed Lookup: `dig`

For more detailed DNS information, the `dig` command (**Domain Information Groper**) is often preferred by system administrators. It provides much more verbose output, including information about the query itself, the responding DNS server, and various types of DNS records.

```
dig google.com


; <<>> DiG 9.18.12-0ubuntu0.22.04.3-Ubuntu <<>> google.com
;; global options: +cmd
;; Got answer:
;; ->>HEADER<<- opcode: QUERY, status: NOERROR, id: 54321
;; flags: qr rd ra; QUERY: 1, ANSWER: 1, AUTHORITY: 0, ADDITIONAL: 1

;; OPT PSEUDOSECTION:
; EDNS: version: 0, flags:; udp: 65494
;; QUESTION SECTION:
;google.com.                    IN      A

;; ANSWER SECTION:
google.com.            299      IN      A       142.250.179.142

;; Query time: 45 msec
;; SERVER: 127.0.0.53#53(127.0.0.53)
;; WHEN: Thu Jul 25 12:05:10 BST 2024
;; MSG SIZE  rcvd: 55
```

The key part is usually the `ANSWER SECTION`, which shows the record type (`A` for IPv4 address), the time-to-live (TTL in seconds - `299`), and the actual IP address (`142.250.179.142`). `dig` can query for specific record types (like `MX` for mail, `AAAA` for IPv6, `TXT` for text records) using `dig google.com MX`, `dig google.com AAAA`, etc.

Older/Interactive Lookup: `nslookup`

`nslookup` is another tool for querying DNS servers. It's older than `dig` but still widely available. It can be used non-interactively like `host` or `dig`, or interactively where you get an `nslookup` prompt.

```
nslookup google.com

Server:         127.0.0.53
Address:        127.0.0.53#53
```

```
Non-authoritative answer:
Name:    google.com
Address: 142.250.179.142
Name:    google.com
Address: 2a00:1450:4009:824::200e
```

Generally:

- Use `host` for quick, simple lookups (Name -> IP).
- Use `dig` for detailed DNS diagnostics and querying specific record types.
- Use `nslookup` if `dig` isn't available or if you prefer its interactive mode.

Downloading Files from the Web: `wget` and `curl`

Need to download a file from a web or FTP server directly from the command line, without opening a browser? `wget` and `curl` are your tools.

`wget` (World Wide Web Get)

`wget` is a straightforward command-line downloader. Its basic usage is simple: give it the URL of the file you want to download.

```
# Download the homepage of example.com
wget http://example.com
```

By default, `wget` saves the file using the name from the URL (`index.html` in this case) and shows progress information.

```
--2024-07-25 12:15:30--  http://example.com/
Resolving example.com (example.com)... 93.184.216.34,
2606:2800:220:1:248:1893:25c8:1946
Connecting to example.com (example.com)|93.184.216.34|:80... connected.
HTTP request sent, awaiting response... 200 OK
Length: 1256 (1.2K) [text/html]
Saving to: 'index.html'

index.html          100%[===================>]   1.23K  --.-KB/s    in 0s

2024-07-25 12:15:30 (15.0 MB/s) - 'index.html' saved [1256/1256]
```

You can specify the output filename using the -O (uppercase O) option:

```
wget -O example_page.html http://example.com
```

wget is particularly good at recursive downloads (mirroring websites) using options like -r (recursive), -l depth (recursion depth), -np (no parent), but these are more advanced use cases.

curl (Client URL)

curl is an incredibly versatile tool for transferring data with URLs. It supports many protocols (HTTP, HTTPS, FTP, SCP, SFTP, LDAP, etc.) and has a vast array of options, making it a favorite for interacting with web APIs and scripting network requests.

By default, curl prints the content of the URL directly to **standard output (stdout)**:

```
# Display the content of example.com on the terminal
curl http://example.com

<!doctype html>
<html>
<head>
    <title>Example Domain</title>
... (rest of HTML source) ...
</html>
```

To save the output to a file, you can use shell redirection (Chapter 9):

```
curl http://example.com > example_curl.html
```

Alternatively, use curl's options:

- -O (uppercase O): Save the file using the filename from the URL (similar to wget).
- -o filename (lowercase o): Save the file to the specified filename.

```
# Save using filename from URL
curl -O http://example.com/index.html

# Save to a specific name
curl -o example_curl_o.html http://example.com
```

curl is extremely powerful for things like sending custom HTTP headers (-H), using different request methods like POST (-X POST), sending data (-d), handling cookies, following redirects (-L), and much more, making it invaluable for web development and API testing directly from the command line.

wget vs curl **Quick Comparison**

- **wget**: Simpler by default, primarily designed for downloading files and recursive retrieval. Generally better for straightforward downloading tasks.
- **curl**: More versatile, handles more protocols, great for interacting with URLs (displaying, sending data, headers), often preferred for scripting and API interaction.

Both are excellent tools to have in your repertoire.

Secure Remote Connections: ssh (Secure Shell)

How do you securely log into and control another Linux or UNIX machine over a network? The standard answer is **SSH (Secure Shell)**. SSH provides an encrypted connection, protecting your password and all the data transmitted between your local machine and the remote server from eavesdropping. It completely replaced older, insecure protocols like telnet.

Basic Connection

The basic syntax is straightforward:

ssh username@hostname_or_IP

- **username**: The username you want to log in as on the *remote* machine.
- **hostname_or_IP**: The DNS hostname or IP address of the *remote* machine.

```
ssh ada@192.168.1.200
# Or using a hostname if DNS is set up:
ssh ada@remote-server.example.com
```

First-Time Connection: Host Key Verification

The very first time you connect to a specific remote host, SSH will present a message like this:

```
The authenticity of host 'remote-server.example.com (192.168.1.200)' can't be
established.
ED25519 key fingerprint is SHA256:AbCdEfGhIjKlMnOpQrStUvWxYz0123456789aBcDeFg.
Are you sure you want to continue connecting (yes/no/[fingerprint])?
```

This is a security feature. The remote server presents its unique **host key**. SSH asks you to confirm that you trust this key (and therefore, the identity of the server). If you're expecting to connect to this server, type `yes` and press Enter. SSH will store the host key in a file called `~/.ssh/known_hosts` on your *local* machine.

On subsequent connections, SSH will check if the key presented by the server matches the one stored in `known_hosts`. If it matches, the connection proceeds. If it *doesn't* match, SSH will give you a **big scary warning**, suggesting a potential "man-in-the-middle" attack (someone intercepting your connection) or that the server's key has legitimately changed (e.g., after an OS reinstall). Investigate carefully if you see this warning!

Authentication

After host key verification, the server needs to authenticate *you*. The most common method initially is:

- **Password Authentication:** The remote server prompts you for the password associated with the `username` you specified.

    ```
    ada@remote-server.example.com's password:
    ```

    Type the password (it won't be echoed to the screen) and press Enter. If successful, you'll be greeted with the remote machine's shell prompt! You can now run commands on the remote server as if you were sitting in front of it.

    To end the SSH session, simply type `exit` or press `Ctrl+D` at the remote prompt.

- **Public Key Authentication (Brief Mention):** A more secure and often more convenient method involves creating a pair of cryptographic keys (a private key stored securely on your local machine and a public key placed on the remote server). SSH can then authenticate you using these keys without needing a password. Setting this up is beyond the scope of this basic chapter but is highly recommended for regular SSH users.

Secure File Transfer: `scp` and `sftp`

Now that you can log into a remote machine with SSH, how do you securely copy files back and forth? SSH provides the underlying security for two common file transfer commands: `scp` and `sftp`.

`scp` (Secure Copy)

`scp` works very much like the local `cp` command (Chapter 3), but allows you to specify remote locations using the `user@host:` syntax.

1. Copying Local File to Remote Host:

```
scp /path/to/local/file username@hostname:/path/to/remote/destination/
```

```
# Copy my local notes.txt to ada's home directory on remote-server
scp ~/practice_files/notes.txt ada@remote-server.example.com:~/

# Copy a local script into a specific directory on the remote server
scp ~/scripts/deploy.sh ada@remote-server.example.com:/opt/scripts/
```

2. Copying Remote File to Local Host:

```
scp username@hostname:/path/to/remote/file /path/to/local/destination/
```

```
# Copy remote_app.log from remote-server to the current local directory (.)
scp ada@remote-server.example.com:/var/log/remote_app.log .

# Copy a configuration file from remote server to local /tmp directory
scp ada@remote-server.example.com:/etc/config.conf /tmp/
```

3. Copying Directories Recursively:

Just like `cp`, use the `-r` option to copy entire directories:

```
# Copy the local project_files directory to the remote home directory
scp -r ~/tar_practice/project_files/ ada@remote-server.example.com:~/
```

`scp` will typically prompt you for the remote user's password (unless key-based authentication is set up) and show file transfer progress. It's excellent for single file/directory transfers or use within scripts.

`sftp` (Secure File Transfer Protocol)

`sftp` provides an interactive, FTP-like session over an SSH connection. It's useful when you want to browse the remote filesystem, upload/download multiple files, or perform other file management tasks within a single secure session.

Start an `sftp` session:

```
sftp username@hostname
```

You'll authenticate (usually with a password) and then get an `sftp>` prompt:

```
Connected to remote-server.example.com.
sftp>
```

Now you can use various commands that operate within the `sftp` session:

- `ls`, `ll`: List files on the **remote** server.
- `pwd`: Show the current working directory on the **remote** server.
- `cd path`: Change directory on the **remote** server.
- `lcd path`: Change directory on the **local** machine.
- `lpwd`: Show the current working directory on the **local** machine.
- `get remote_file [local_filename]`: Download `remote_file` to the local machine.
- `put local_file [remote_filename]`: Upload `local_file` to the remote machine.
- `mkdir directory_name`: Create a directory on the **remote** server.
- `rm remote_file`: Delete a file on the **remote** server.
- `help`: Display available `sftp` commands.
- `quit` or `exit`: End the sftp session.

```
sftp> pwd
Remote working directory: /home/ada
sftp> ls
backups        notes.txt      project_files
sftp> lcd ~/Downloads
Local working directory: /home/ada/Downloads
sftp> get notes.txt
Fetching /home/ada/notes.txt to notes.txt
/home/ada/notes.txt                      100%   13     0.1KB/s   00:00
sftp> put important_local_data.csv
Uploading important_local_data.csv to /home/ada/important_local_data.csv
important_local_data.csv                 100%   512    4.7KB/s   00:00
sftp> quit
```

`sftp` is great for interactive file management over a secure connection.

Chapter Summary

This chapter equipped you with the essential command-line tools for interacting with networks. You learned how to check your system's network interfaces and IP addresses using `ip addr` (and the older `ifconfig`). We practiced testing basic connectivity to other hosts with `ping`. You saw how to inspect your system's routing table using `ip route` and how to translate domain names to IP addresses using DNS query tools like `host`, `dig`, and `nslookup`. We explored downloading files from the web using the straightforward `wget` and the versatile `curl`. Crucially, you learned how to establish secure remote shell sessions using `ssh` and transfer files securely using `scp` (for direct copying) and `sftp` (for interactive sessions).

These networking commands are fundamental for diagnostics, remote administration, and accessing online resources directly from your terminal. Many of these tools become even more powerful when combined within scripts to automate tasks. In the next chapter, we'll finally bring together much of what you've learned by diving into the world of shell scripting, allowing you to write your own simple programs to automate your command-line workflows.

Chapter 15: Writing Your First Shell Scripts

You've journeyed deep into the Linux command line, mastering navigation, file manipulation, process management, permissions, and even networking basics. You're comfortable running individual commands and piping them together (Chapter 9). Now, it's time to take the next logical step: **automation**. What if you could bundle a sequence of commands into a single file and execute them all with one instruction? What if you could make your command sequences smarter, allowing them to make decisions or repeat tasks? Welcome to the world of **shell scripting**! This chapter will guide you through writing your very first scripts using the Bash shell, combining the commands you already know with basic programming concepts to automate tasks and enhance your efficiency.

What is Shell Scripting? Automating Tasks

At its core, a **shell script** is simply a plain text file containing a sequence of shell commands. Instead of typing these commands one by one at the prompt, you write them into a file, and then tell the shell to execute that file. The shell reads the file line by line, executing each command just as if you had typed it interactively.

Why bother writing scripts?

- **Automation:** Eliminate repetitive typing for common command sequences.
- **Consistency:** Ensure complex tasks are performed the same way every time, reducing errors.
- **Efficiency:** Execute multiple commands with a single instruction.
- **Customization:** Create your own custom commands tailored to your specific needs.
- **Sharing:** Easily share workflows and procedures with others.

Think of it like writing a detailed recipe or a to-do list for the shell. Instead of telling it each small step individually every time, you give it the whole list at once, and it carries out the instructions faithfully.

Creating a Simple Script

Let's create our first script. It won't do much yet, but it will illustrate the basic process.

Choosing an Editor

You'll need a text editor to write your script. As we discussed in Chapter 6, `nano` is a great beginner-friendly choice, or you can use the more powerful `vim` if you've started learning it. Any plain text editor will work.

The Shebang (`#!/bin/bash`)

The very first line of almost every shell script you write should be the **shebang**. It looks like this:

```
#!/bin/bash
```

- `#`: Normally indicates a comment (which we'll discuss later), but when it's the *very first* character pair `#!`, it has a special meaning.
- `!`: This pair `#!` is the "shebang" or "hashbang".
- `/bin/bash`: This is the absolute path to the interpreter program that should be used to execute the rest of the commands in the file.

The shebang tells the Linux kernel, "Don't just run this file directly; instead, run the program located at `/bin/bash`, and feed this script file to it as input." This ensures your script is executed by the Bash shell, even if the user running it has a different default shell. While other interpreters exist (`#!/bin/sh`, `#!/usr/bin/python`), `/bin/bash` is the standard shebang for Bash scripts.

Writing Simple Commands

Let's create a script called `hello_world.sh`. Open your editor:

```
nano hello_world.sh
```

Now, enter the following lines:

```
#!/bin/bash

# My first shell script

echo "Hello, Linux World!"
echo "The current directory is:"
pwd
echo "The directory contains:"
ls
```

Save the file and exit the editor (Ctrl+O, Enter, Ctrl+X in nano).

Making Scripts Executable

You've created the script file, but if you try to run it directly right now, you'll likely get a "Permission denied" error (as we learned about permissions in Chapter 7). By default, new text files do not have execute permission.

```
# This will probably fail
hello_world.sh

bash: hello_world.sh: command not found
# Or potentially:
bash: ./hello_world.sh: Permission denied
```

File Permissions Recap

Remember ls -l shows permissions? Let's check our new script:

```
ls -l hello_world.sh

-rw-r--r-- 1 ada ada 110 Jul 25 14:10 hello_world.sh
```

Notice the lack of x (execute) permissions in the string -rw-r--r--. We need to add it for the user owner (u).

Using chmod +x

The chmod command is used to change permissions. The +x option adds execute permission.

```
chmod +x hello_world.sh

# Verify the change
ls -l hello_world.sh


-rwxr-xr-x 1 ada ada 110 Jul 25 14:10 hello_world.sh
```

Now the x is present for the user owner!

Running Scripts

With execute permission set, you can now run your script. There are two main ways:

Using the Path (./script_name)

Even though the script is executable, if you just type `hello_world.sh`, the shell likely won't find it. This is because, for security reasons, the current directory (`.`) is usually **not** included in the `$PATH` environment variable (which we discussed in Chapter 11). The shell only looks for commands in the directories listed in `$PATH`.

To run an executable in the current directory, you must explicitly tell the shell where it is by prefixing the script name with `./` (which means "in the current directory"):

```
./hello_world.sh
```

The shell now finds the script, reads the `#!/bin/bash` shebang, executes it using Bash, and you see the output:

```
Hello, Linux World!
The current directory is:
/home/ada/scripting_practice # Or wherever you created the script
The directory contains:
hello_world.sh
```

Running with the Interpreter (bash script_name)

Alternatively, you can explicitly tell Bash to run the script, even if it doesn't have execute permission set. In this case, the shebang line is actually ignored, because you're already specifying the interpreter.

```
# Let's remove execute permission first to demonstrate
```

```
chmod -x hello_world.sh

# Now run it with bash explicitly
bash hello_world.sh
```

You'll get the same output as before. This method is useful if you can't change the permissions of a script file (perhaps you don't own it) but you still want to run it. However, using `./script_name` after setting execute permission is the more standard way to run your own scripts.

Using Variables in Scripts

Just like in the interactive shell (Chapter 11), variables are essential in scripts for storing and reusing information. The syntax is the same: `variable=value` (no spaces!) and `$variable` to access the value.

Let's create a script `user_info.sh` that uses variables:

```
#!/bin/bash

# Script demonstrating variable usage

# Static variable
greeting="Welcome"

# Variable assigned from command output (Command Substitution)
current_user=$(whoami)
current_dir=$(pwd)

# Displaying info
echo "$greeting, $current_user!"
echo "You are currently in the directory: $current_dir"
```

Make it executable (`chmod +x user_info.sh`) and run it (`./user_info.sh`):

```
Welcome, ada!
You are currently in the directory: /home/ada/scripting_practice
```

Command Substitution

Notice the $(whoami) and $(pwd) syntax in the previous script. This is **command substitution**. It allows you to capture the standard output of a command and use it as part of another command or assign it to a variable.

- $(command): This is the modern, preferred syntax. The command inside the parentheses is executed, and its standard output replaces the entire $(...) expression.
- `command` (Backticks): This is the older syntax. It works similarly but has some quoting complexities and doesn't nest as easily as $(). It's better to use $() unless you need compatibility with very old shells.

Command substitution is incredibly useful for getting dynamic information into your scripts, like the current date, hostname, disk usage, or results from other tools.

```
#!/bin/bash

# Demonstrating command substitution

today=$(date +%Y-%m-%d) # Get date in YYYY-MM-DD format
files_in_dir=$(ls | wc -l) # Count files in current directory

echo "Today's date is: $today"
echo "There are $files_in_dir item(s) in this directory."
```

Reading User Input: read

So far, our scripts run non-interactively. What if you want the script to ask the user for information while it's running? The read command pauses the script, waits for the user to type something on standard input (usually the keyboard) and press Enter, and then stores the input into one or more shell variables.

Basic read

```
#!/bin/bash

# Simple read example

echo "Please enter your name:"
read user_name # Reads input and stores it in the variable 'user_name'
echo "Hello, $user_name! Nice to meet you."
```

164

Run this script (`chmod +x` first). It will pause after the first `echo`, waiting for your input. Type your name, press Enter, and it will continue.

```
Please enter your name:
Ada Lovelace # You type this
Hello, Ada Lovelace! Nice to meet you.
```

Prompting with `read -p`

Typing the prompt with `echo` first works, but `read` has a `-p` option to display a prompt string directly, without needing a separate `echo` and without adding a newline after the prompt:

```
#!/bin/bash

# Using read -p for a prompt

read -p "What is your favorite Linux distribution? " fav_distro
echo "$fav_distro is a great choice!"
```

Run it:

```
What is your favorite Linux distribution? Arch Linux # You type this
Arch Linux is a great choice!
```

Basic Control Flow

Now we get into making scripts "smarter". Control flow structures allow your script to make decisions (`if` statements) or repeat actions (`for` and `while` loops).

Conditional Statements (`if`)

`if` statements let your script execute different blocks of commands based on whether a certain **condition** is true or false.

Syntax:

```
if condition; then
  # Commands to run if condition is true
elif another_condition; then
  # Commands to run if the first condition was false
  # AND another_condition is true
```

```
else
    # Commands to run if ALL preceding conditions were false
fi # Marks the end of the if statement
```

The `elif` (else if) and `else` parts are optional. You can have multiple `elif` blocks.

How are Conditions Evaluated? The `test` Command and `[[ ]]`

How does the `if` statement know if a condition is true or false? In shell scripting, conditions are typically evaluated using other commands that return an **exit status** (which we'll discuss more soon). An exit status of **0** means **success (true)**, and any non-zero exit status means **failure (false)**.

- `test expression` or `[ expression ]`: The traditional way. `[` is actually a command (a synonym for `test`). **Spaces around the brackets and inside separating operators are mandatory!**
- `[[ expression ]]`: An enhanced Bash-specific version. It's generally safer (less prone to errors with word splitting and pathname expansion) and offers more features (like pattern matching with == and regular expression matching with =~). **Spaces inside are still required.** For Bash scripting, `[[ ... ]]` is usually recommended over `[ ... ]`.

Common Tests (within `[[ ... ]]`):

- **File Tests:**
  - `-e file`: True if `file` exists.
  - `-f file`: True if `file` exists and is a regular file.
  - `-d file`: True if `file` exists and is a directory.
  - `-r file`: True if `file` exists and is readable.
  - `-w file`: True if `file` exists and is writable.
  - `-x file`: True if `file` exists and is executable.
  - `-s file`: True if `file` exists and has a size greater than zero.
- **String Comparisons:**
  - `string1 == string2` or `string1 = string2`: True if strings are identical. (Use quotes around variables: `[[ "$var" == "value" ]]`)
  - `string1 != string2`: True if strings are not identical.
  - `-z string`: True if `string` is empty (zero length).
  - `-n string`: True if `string` is not empty.
- **Numeric Comparisons:** (Use these inside `[[ ... ]]` or with `test/[ ... ]`)
  - `num1 -eq num2`: Equal.
  - `num1 -ne num2`: Not equal.

- num1 `-gt` num2: Greater than.
- num1 `-ge` num2: Greater than or equal to.
- num1 `-lt` num2: Less than.
- num1 `-le` num2: Less than or equal to.
- **Logical Operators (within** `[[ ... ]]`**):**
  - `&&`: Logical AND (condition1 && condition2)
  - `||`: Logical OR (condition1 || condition2)
  - `!`: Logical NOT (! condition)

Example `if` Script:

```bash
#!/bin/bash

# Simple if/else example

read -p "Enter a number: " number

if [[ "$number" -gt 100 ]]; then
  echo "That's a big number!"
elif [[ "$number" -lt 10 ]]; then
  echo "That's a small number."
else
  echo "That number is between 10 and 100 (inclusive)."
fi


# Check if a file exists
filename="hello_world.sh"
if [[ -f "$filename" ]]; then
  echo "$filename exists and is a regular file."
else
  echo "$filename does not exist or is not a regular file."
fi
```

Simple Loops (`for` and `while`)

Loops allow you to repeat a block of commands multiple times.

`for` Loop (Iterating over a list):

The `for` loop executes commands once for each item in a given list.

Syntax:

```bash
for variable_name in item1 item2 item3 ... ; do
  # Commands to execute, using $variable_name
```

```
done
```

Example for Script:

```bash
#!/bin/bash

# Basic for loop example

echo "Processing files:"
for file in notes.txt hello_world.sh user_info.sh; do
  echo " -> Found file: $file"
  # We could do something else with $file here, like backup or check it
done

echo ""
echo "Counting from 1 to 5:"
# Brace expansion creates the list {1..5} -> 1 2 3 4 5
for i in {1..5}; do
  echo "Number $i"
done
```

while Loop (Executing while a condition is true):

The while loop keeps executing commands as long as its condition evaluates to true (exit status 0).

Syntax:

```
while condition; do
  # Commands to execute
  # IMPORTANT: Something inside the loop must eventually
  # make the condition false, otherwise it's an infinite loop!
done
```

Example while Script:

```bash
#!/bin/bash

# Basic while loop example

counter=1
max_count=5

echo "While loop counting:"
```

```
while [[ "$counter" -le "$max_count" ]]; do
  echo "Counter is now $counter"
  # Increment the counter (using arithmetic expansion $((...)) )
  counter=$((counter + 1))
done
```

Loops are fundamental for processing multiple files, reading data line by line, or performing actions a specific number of times.

Positional Parameters ($1, $2, ...)

How can you provide input to your script *when you run it* on the command line, rather than interactively using read? You pass arguments, and the script accesses them using special variables called **positional parameters**.

When you run a script like ./myscript argument1 data.txt 100, the shell makes these arguments available inside the script:

- $0: The name of the script itself (e.g., ./myscript).
- $1: The first argument (argument1).
- $2: The second argument (data.txt).
- $3: The third argument (100).
- $...: Up to $9.
- ${10}, ${11}, ...: For arguments beyond the 9th (use curly braces).
- $#: Contains the *number* of arguments passed to the script (excluding $0).
- $*: Expands to a single string containing all arguments joined by the first character of the IFS (Internal Field Separator) variable (usually a space). "$*" is like "$1 $2 $3".
- $@: Similar to $*, but when quoted ("$@"), it expands to separate words: "$1" "$2" "$3". This is usually safer and more useful, especially when looping through arguments that might contain spaces.

Example Script Using Arguments:

```
#!/bin/bash

# Script demonstrating positional parameters

echo "The script name is: $0"
echo "The first argument is: $1"
echo "The second argument is: $2"
echo "The total number of arguments is: $#"
```

```
echo "All arguments (using \$@): $@"

# Check if a filename was provided as the first argument
if [[ -f "$1" ]]; then
  echo "Processing file: $1"
  # Add commands to process the file here
else
  echo "Warning: File '$1' not found or not provided."
fi
```

Save this as `arg_script.sh`, make it executable, and run it with arguments:

```
./arg_script.sh important_data.log report.pdf

The script name is: ./arg_script.sh
The first argument is: important_data.log
The second argument is: report.pdf
The total number of arguments is: 2
All arguments (using $@): important_data.log report.pdf
Warning: File 'important_data.log' not found or not provided. # Assuming it
doesn't exist
```

Positional parameters make your scripts much more flexible, allowing them to operate on different data or with different options each time they are run.

Exit Status ($?)

Every command you run finishes with an **exit status** (or return code), which is an integer value indicating whether the command executed successfully or encountered an error.

- **Exit Status 0**: Conventionally means **success**.
- **Exit Status Non-Zero (1-255)**: Conventionally means **failure**. Different non-zero values can signify different types of errors, though this depends on the specific command.

The shell stores the exit status of the *most recently executed foreground command* in the special variable $?.

```
# Run a successful command
ls hello_world.sh
# Output: hello_world.sh
echo $? # Check exit status
```

```
# Output: 0 (success)

# Run a command that fails
ls non_existent_file.txt
# Output: ls: cannot access 'non_existent_file.txt': No such file or directory
echo $? # Check exit status
# Output: 2 (or some other non-zero value indicating failure)
```

You can use $? within your scripts, especially in if statements, to check if a crucial command succeeded before proceeding.

```
#!/bin/bash

# Checking exit status

grep "some_pattern" data.file

if [[ "$?" -ne 0 ]]; then
  echo "Error: grep command failed to find the pattern or read the file."
  # Maybe exit the script here
fi

echo "Grep finished, proceeding..."
```

You can also explicitly set the exit status of your *own* script using the exit command followed by a number. exit 0 signals success, while exit 1 (or another non-zero number) signals failure. This is useful for indicating the outcome of your script to other scripts or processes that might call it.

```
#!/bin/bash

# Setting exit status

read -p "Enter filename: " file

if [[ ! -f "$file" ]]; then
  echo "Error: File '$file' not found." >&2 # Write error to stderr
  exit 1 # Exit with failure status
fi

echo "File '$file' found. Processing..."
# ... process the file ...
exit 0 # Exit with success status
```

Adding Comments (#)

As scripts get more complex, it's vital to add **comments** to explain *what* the script does, *why* certain commands are used, or *how* a particular section works. Comments make your scripts understandable to others (and to your future self!).

In Bash, any text on a line following a hash symbol (#) is treated as a comment and ignored by the shell (unless it's the shebang #! on the very first line).

```
#!/bin/bash

# ===============================================
# Simple Backup Script
# Author: Your Name
# Date:   2024-07-25
# ===============================================

# Configuration Variables (Set these!)
SOURCE_DIR="/home/ada/Documents" # Directory to back up
TARGET_DIR="/mnt/backup_drive/daily" # Where to store the backup
FILENAME="docs_backup_$(date +%Y%m%d_%H%M%S).tar.gz" # Backup filename with
timestamp

# Check if target directory exists (using file test from 'if' section)
if [[ ! -d "$TARGET_DIR" ]]; then
  echo "Error: Target directory '$TARGET_DIR' not found." >&2 # Error to stderr
  exit 1 # Exit with error code
fi

# Create the compressed archive (using tar from Chapter 12)
echo "Starting backup of $SOURCE_DIR to $TARGET_DIR/$FILENAME..."
tar -czf "$TARGET_DIR/$FILENAME" "$SOURCE_DIR"

# Check the exit status of the tar command
if [[ "$?" -eq 0 ]]; then
  echo "Backup completed successfully!"
  exit 0 # Success
else
  echo "Error: Backup failed!" >&2
  exit 2 # Exit with a different error code
fi
```

Use comments liberally to document your code. It's one of the hallmarks of a good script.

Chapter Summary

This chapter unlocked the power of automation by introducing you to Bash shell scripting. You learned that a script is a text file of commands, starting with the crucial **shebang** (#!/bin/bash). We covered making scripts executable using chmod +x and running them via ./script_name. You saw how to use **variables**, capture command output with **command substitution** $(), and make scripts interactive by reading user input with read. We explored fundamental **control flow**: making decisions with if/ elif/else statements (using conditions tested via [[...]]) and repeating commands with for and while loops. You learned how to pass arguments to scripts using **positional parameters** ($1, $2, $#, $@) and how to check command success using the **exit status** variable $?, as well as setting your script's own exit status with exit. Finally, we emphasized the importance of adding explanatory **comments** (#) to make your scripts understandable.

You now have the basic building blocks to automate tasks and create your own simple command-line tools. This is just the beginning of shell scripting; it's a deep and powerful subject. In the next chapter, we'll look at some more advanced command-line tools and techniques, often used within scripts or for complex data manipulation, including sed, awk, xargs, and terminal multiplexers.

Chapter 16: Power Tools and Techniques

You've built a solid foundation. You can script basic automation (Chapter 15), manage your files and processes, and navigate the network. Now, let's add some specialized, high-powered tools to your command-line arsenal. These utilities are often the secret ingredients in sophisticated scripts or elegant one-liner commands that manipulate data in complex ways. We'll explore `xargs` for turning input lines into command arguments, the stream editor `sed` for automated text modifications, the pattern-processing language `awk` for dissecting text data, `diff` for comparing files, `wc`, `sort`, and `uniq` for counting and organizing data, and finally, get a brief introduction to terminal multiplexers like `screen` and `tmux` for managing persistent sessions. These tools significantly expand the scope of what you can achieve directly from the terminal.

Processing Input with `xargs`

Remember pipes (|) from Chapter 9? They are fantastic for feeding the standard output of one command into the standard input of another. However, some commands don't primarily read from standard input; instead, they expect their input as *command-line arguments*. For instance, `rm` takes filenames as arguments, `echo` prints its arguments, and `cp` needs source and destination arguments.

What if you have a list of filenames (perhaps generated by `find` or `ls`) on standard input, and you want to pass those filenames as arguments to `rm` or `cp`? This is where `xargs` (extend **arg**uments) comes in. It reads items (usually lines) from standard input and executes a specified command, using those items as arguments.

Think of `xargs` as a bridge or a conveyor belt adapter. It takes items arriving on the standard input belt and places them into the argument hopper of another command machine.

Basic Usage

Let's see a simple example. Suppose we want echo to print three separate filenames:

```
# Create some dummy files first
touch file1.txt file2.log file3.sh

# Use ls to generate the list, pipe it to xargs, which runs echo
ls file* | xargs echo "Processing:"
```

xargs reads "file1.txt", "file2.log", and "file3.sh" from its standard input (provided by ls) and then runs the command echo "Processing:" file1.txt file2.log file3.sh.

```
Processing: file1.txt file2.log file3.sh
```

Without xargs, if you piped directly to echo, it would treat the entire input as a single block of text (if echo even read stdin, which it often doesn't in this context). xargs breaks the input into items (by default, separated by whitespace or newlines) and passes them as distinct arguments.

Working with find

One of the most classic and powerful uses of xargs is in combination with the find command (Chapter 10). find is great at locating files based on complex criteria, and xargs lets you perform actions on those found files efficiently.

Let's say we want to remove all files ending in .bak in our home directory's subdirectories. We could use find ... -exec rm {} \;, but xargs can sometimes be more efficient, especially for a large number of files, because it can pass multiple filenames to a single rm command invocation (similar to find ... -exec ... +).

```
# Find .bak files and pipe the list to xargs, which runs rm
find . -name "*.bak" -type f | xargs rm -v
```

A Critical Problem: Filenames with Spaces

The command above works fine for simple filenames. But what if you have filenames containing spaces, newlines, or quotes? The default behavior of xargs (splitting by whitespace) will break.

```
# Create a problematic filename
touch "a file with spaces.bak"
```

```
# Try the previous find command (this will likely FAIL or error)
find . -name "*.bak" -type f | xargs rm -v
```

xargs will likely see "a", "file", "with", "spaces.bak" as separate arguments, leading `rm` to complain it can't find files named "a", "file", etc.

The Safe Solution: `find -print0` **and** `xargs -0`

To handle *any* possible character in filenames safely, use this robust combination:

- `find ... -print0`: This tells `find` to print the matching filenames separated by a **null character** instead of a newline. The null character is the one character guaranteed never to appear in a valid Linux filename.
- `xargs -0`: This tells `xargs` to expect its input items to be separated by **null characters** instead of whitespace or newlines.

```
# Safely find and remove .bak files, even with weird names
find . -name "*.bak" -type f -print0 | xargs -0 rm -v
```

This `find ... -print0 | xargs -0 ...` pattern is the **recommended way** to pipe filenames from `find` to `xargs` to ensure safe handling of all possible filenames.

`xargs` has other useful options like `-p` (prompt before executing each command) and `-n max_args` (use at most `max_args` items per command line). Check `man xargs` for details.

Stream Editing with `sed`

Often, you need to perform simple, repetitive text transformations on a file or a stream of data – for example, replacing all occurrences of one word with another, deleting lines containing a specific pattern, or inserting text before certain lines. The `sed` command (stream **ed**itor) is designed for exactly this.

Unlike interactive editors like `nano` or `vim`, `sed` is non-interactive. You provide it with a script of editing commands (often just a single command), and it reads input line by line, applies the command(s) to each line, and prints the potentially modified line to standard output. It doesn't modify the original file unless you explicitly tell it to (using the `-i` option, use with caution!).

Think of `sed` as an automated text-processing robot on an assembly line. It inspects each item (line) passing by, performs a predefined modification (like swapping a part or removing a defect), and sends the result down the line (to standard output).

Basic Substitution (s/.../.../)

The most common `sed` command is substitution, using the s command:

```
's/PATTERN/REPLACEMENT/FLAGS'
```

- s: Indicates the substitute command.
- /: A delimiter character (slash is traditional, but any character not in PATTERN or REPLACEMENT can be used, e.g., s#PATTERN#REPLACEMENT#).
- PATTERN: The text string or regular expression to search for.
- REPLACEMENT: The string to replace the matched pattern with.
- FLAGS: Optional flags that modify the behavior. The most common is:
  - g (global): Replace *all* occurrences of PATTERN on the line, not just the first one.

Let's try replacing "blue" with "scarlet" in our `poem.txt` (from Chapter 4):

```
# Print modified lines to stdout, poem.txt remains unchanged
sed 's/blue/scarlet/' poem.txt


Roses are red,
Violets are scarlet,
Linux is awesome, and so are you!
```

If a line had "blue blue sky", only the first "blue" would be replaced without the g flag. With g:

```
echo "blue blue sky" | sed 's/blue/red/g'

red red sky
```

Applying sed

You can apply `sed` commands in two main ways:

1. **To Files:** sed 'script' filename(s)

   ```
   sed 's/red/cyan/' poem.txt
   ```

2. **In Pipelines:** `command | sed 'script'`

```
ls -l | sed 's/ada/alex/' # Replace 'ada' with 'alex' in ls output
```

Other Basic `sed` Commands

- **Deleting Lines** (d): Delete lines matching a pattern.

```
# Print poem.txt, but delete lines containing 'Violets'
sed '/Violets/d' poem.txt

Roses are red,
Linux is awesome, and so are you!
```

- **Address Ranges:** You can apply commands only to specific lines or ranges (e.g., `sed '1,2d' file` deletes lines 1 and 2; `sed '/start_pattern/,/end_pattern/s/foo/bar/' file` substitutes only between lines matching start and end patterns).

`sed` is incredibly powerful, especially when combined with regular expressions. It can perform complex transformations, but for simple substitutions and deletions, the `s` and `d` commands are your starting point. Remember to consult `man sed` for its extensive capabilities. For quick interactive editing, use `nano` or `vim`; for automated stream editing, use `sed`.

Text Processing with awk

While `sed` operates on the entire line, `awk` excels at processing text data that is structured into **fields** or columns. It reads input line by line, splits each line into fields based on a delimiter (whitespace by default), and allows you to perform actions based on patterns or field values. It's essentially a data extraction and reporting tool and even a small programming language. Its name comes from the initials of its creators: Alfred **A**ho, Peter **W**einberger, and Brian **K**ernighan.

Think of `awk` like a programmable spreadsheet for your terminal. It processes data row by row (lines) and lets you easily manipulate or extract specific columns (fields).

Basic Structure: `pattern { action }`

An `awk` program consists of a sequence of `pattern { action }` pairs. For each input line:

1. awk checks if the line matches the pattern.
2. If it matches (or if no pattern is provided, which matches every line), awk executes the action block (commands within curly braces {}).
3. If no action is provided, the default action is to print the entire matching line (print $0).

Field-Based Processing

This is awk's superpower. When it reads a line, it automatically splits it into fields based on the **Field Separator** (FS). By default, FS is any sequence of whitespace (spaces or tabs). Inside the action block, you can refer to these fields using special variables:

- $0: The entire input line.
- $1: The first field.
- $2: The second field.
- $...: Subsequent fields.
- $NF: The value of the **N**umber of **F**ields (i.e., the *last* field on the line).

Let's use ls -l output, which is nicely column-based (though spacing can vary):

```
ls -l


total 24
-rw-r--r-- 1 ada users   13 Jul 25 10:14 notes.txt
drwxr-xr-x 3 ada users 4096 Jul 25 10:14 project_files
-rw-r--r-- 1 ada users  235 Jul 25 10:34 my_project.tar.gz
```

Now, let's use awk to print only the permissions (field 1) and the filename (field 9):

```
ls -l | awk '{print $1, $9}'

total
-rw-r--r-- notes.txt
drwxr-xr-x project_files
-rw-r--r-- my_project.tar.gz
```

(Notice awk *processed the "total" line too. We could add a pattern to skip it, e.g.,* awk 'NR > 1 {print $1, $9}' *where* NR *is the record/line number)*

Changing the Field Separator (-F)

What if your data isn't separated by spaces, but by commas, colons, or tabs? Use the -F option *before* the awk script to specify the delimiter.

Consider the /etc/passwd file, where fields are separated by colons (:):

```
root:x:0:0:root:/root:/bin/bash
daemon:x:1:1:daemon:/usr/sbin:/usr/sbin/nologin
bin:x:2:2:bin:/bin:/usr/sbin/nologin
ada:x:1000:1000:Ada Lovelace,,,:/home/ada:/bin/bash
```

Let's print the username (field 1) and the home directory (field 6) for each user:

```
awk -F':' '{print "User:", $1, " Home:", $6}' /etc/passwd

User:  root   Home: /root
User:  daemon  Home: /usr/sbin
User:  bin  Home: /bin
User:  ada  Home: /home/ada
```

awk can also perform calculations, use patterns to select lines (e.g., /pattern/ {action} or $3 > 100 {action}), and has built-in variables (NR for record number, NF for number of fields) and functions. It's a complete programming language, but its most common use is extracting and formatting data based on fields. Explore man awk to see its full potential.

Comparing Files: diff

Have you ever had two versions of a configuration file or a script and wanted to see exactly what changed between them? The diff command is designed for this. It compares two files line by line and outputs a description of the differences required to make the first file identical to the second file.

Think of diff as the change-tracking feature in a word processor, but for plain text files on the command line.

Basic Usage

```
# Create two slightly different files
echo -e "Line 1\nLine 2\nLine 3" > fileA.txt
echo -e "Line 1\nLine Two\nLine 3\nLine 4" > fileB.txt
```

```
# Compare them
diff fileA.txt fileB.txt
```

The default output format can be a bit cryptic:

```
2c2
< Line 2
---
> Line Two
3a4
> Line 4
```

This output describes the changes needed to turn `fileA.txt` into `fileB.txt`:

- 2c2: Line 2 in file A needs to be changed to line 2 in file B.
- `< Line 2`: Shows the line from file A (< means from the first file).
- `---`: Separator.
- `> Line Two`: Shows the corresponding line from file B (> means from the second file).
- 3a4: After line 3 in file A, you need to add line 4 from file B.
- `> Line 4`: Shows the line to be added from file B.

Unified Format (-u)

The default format is okay, but the **unified** format, generated with the -u option, is generally much easier to read and is the standard format for creating patches (files that describe changes).

```
diff -u fileA.txt fileB.txt

--- fileA.txt   2024-07-25 15:10:00.000000000 +0100
+++ fileB.txt   2024-07-25 15:10:15.000000000 +0100
@@ -1,3 +1,4 @@
 Line 1
-Line 2
+Line Two
 Line 3
+Line 4
```

- `--- fileA.txt ...`: Header for the first file.
- `+++ fileB.txt ...`: Header for the second file.

- @@ -1,3 +1,4 @@: A "hunk" header. Shows the line numbers and counts affected in file A (-1,3 means starting at line 1, 3 lines shown) and file B (+1,4 means starting at line 1, 4 lines shown).
- Lines starting with a space ( ): Common lines, present in both files.
- Lines starting with -: Lines present only in the first file (removed).
- Lines starting with +: Lines present only in the second file (added).

This format clearly highlights the differences in context.

Other useful `diff` options include -i (ignore case differences) and -w (ignore whitespace differences). `diff` is essential for tracking changes in code, configuration, or any text-based data.

Counting Things: wc

We've used wc (word count) in pipelines before, but let's look at it properly. Its job is simple: count lines, words, and bytes (or characters) in its input.

Basic Usage

You can give wc filenames as arguments, or pipe data to it.

```
# Count lines, words, and bytes in poem.txt
wc poem.txt

 3  14  75 poem.txt
```

(Output: 3 lines, 14 words, 75 bytes)

```
# Count just the lines in multiple files
wc -l fileA.txt fileB.txt poem.txt

   3 fileA.txt
   4 fileB.txt
   3 poem.txt
  10 total
```

```
# Count the number of files listed by ls in the current directory
ls | wc -l
```

Common Options

- **-l**: Count lines.
- **-w**: Count words (sequences of non-whitespace characters).
- **-c**: Count characters (or cytes - depends on locale).
- **-m**: Count characters, correctly handling multi-byte characters (often preferred over -c for character counts).

wc is a simple but frequently used utility, especially in scripts and pipelines for summarizing data size.

Sorting Data: `sort`

Need to arrange lines of text alphabetically or numerically? The `sort` command does exactly that. It reads lines from files or standard input, sorts them, and writes the result to standard output.

Basic Usage

```
# Create a file with unsorted names
echo "Charlie" > names.txt
echo "Alice" >> names.txt
echo "Bob" >> names.txt
echo "alice" >> names.txt

# Sort the file alphabetically (case-sensitive by default)
sort names.txt

Alice
Bob
Charlie
alice
```

(Notice 'Alice' comes before 'alice' in default ASCII sort order)

```
# Pipe output to sort
ls /etc | sort
```

Common Options

- **-r**: Reverse the sort order (descending).
- **-n**: Perform a numeric sort instead of alphabetic (treats lines as numbers).
- **-f**: Fold lowercase to uppercase for sorting (case-insensitive).

```
sort -f names.txt

Alice
alice
Bob
Charlie
```

- -k field_number: Sort based on a specific key field. Fields are separated by whitespace by default (can be changed with -t). For example, sort -k 3n file.txt sorts numerically based on the 3rd field.
- -u: Unique. Output only the first instance of identical lines. This is equivalent to piping the output through uniq.

```
sort -u names.txt

Alice
Bob
Charlie
alice
```

sort is fundamental for organizing data before processing it further, especially before using uniq.

Removing Duplicates: uniq

The uniq command filters *adjacent*, identical lines from its input, outputting only one copy.

Crucial Point: uniq **only compares adjacent lines**. This means the input *must* be sorted first for uniq to find all duplicate lines across the entire input. The most common pattern is sort file | uniq.

```
# Create a file with adjacent and non-adjacent duplicates
echo "apple" > fruits.txt
echo "banana" >> fruits.txt
echo "apple" >> fruits.txt
echo "orange" >> fruits.txt
echo "banana" >> fruits.txt
echo "banana" >> fruits.txt

# Run uniq directly - doesn't catch the first 'apple' or 'banana'
uniq fruits.txt
```

```
apple
banana
apple
orange
banana
```

Now, sort first, then use uniq:

```
sort fruits.txt | uniq
```

```
apple
banana
orange
```

Common Options

- -c: **C**ount. Precede each output line with the number of times it occurred consecutively in the input.

    ```
    sort fruits.txt | uniq -c
    ```

    ```
        2 apple
        3 banana
        1 orange
    ```

- -d: Only print **d**uplicate lines (lines that appeared more than once consecutively).

    ```
    sort fruits.txt | uniq -d
    ```

    ```
    apple
    banana
    ```

- -u: Only print **u**nique lines (lines that appeared exactly once consecutively).

    ```
    sort fruits.txt | uniq -u
    ```

    ```
    orange
    ```

The sort | uniq combination is indispensable for de-duplicating lists, counting frequencies, and data cleaning.

Terminal Multiplexers: `screen` or `tmux` (Brief Introduction)

Imagine you're logged into a remote server via SSH (Chapter 14) and start a long-running process (like a backup or a complex calculation). What happens if your network connection drops or you accidentally close your SSH window? The process likely gets terminated! Also, wouldn't it be nice to have multiple independent shell sessions accessible within that single SSH connection, like having multiple tabs in one terminal window?

Terminal multiplexers solve these problems. They create persistent sessions that run independently of your SSH connection or terminal window. You can detach from a session, log out, log back in later, and reattach to the session exactly where you left off, with all your programs still running. They also allow you to create multiple "windows" or "panes" (split views) within a single session.

The two most popular multiplexers are `screen` (older, extremely widespread) and `tmux` (newer, highly configurable, often preferred by power users). While their specific commands and keybindings differ, the core concepts are similar.

Think of a multiplexer like a virtual terminal control room. You can start projects (sessions) in different rooms. Each room can have multiple screens (windows/panes). You can leave the control room entirely (detach), and the projects keep running. When you come back (reattach), everything is as you left it.

Key Concepts (Conceptual Overview)

1. **Starting a Session:** You start a new session, often giving it a name for easier identification.

   - `screen`
   - `tmux new-session -s session_name`

2. **Running Commands:** Inside the session, you just use the shell as normal. Start your long-running processes, open editors, etc.

3. **Detaching:** This is the magic. You disconnect your *current* terminal view from the session, but the session and all processes within it **continue running in the background.**

   - screen: Press `Ctrl+A` then `d` (for detach).
   - tmux: Press `Ctrl+B` then `d`.

4. **Listing Sessions:** See which sessions are currently running in the background.

- `screen -ls`
- `tmux ls`

5. **Reattaching:** Connect your terminal back to an existing background session.

   - `screen -r` (or `screen -r session_id`)
   - `tmux attach-session -t session_name` (or `tmux attach -t session_id`)

6. **Multiple Windows/Panes:** Both allow you to create new shell prompts within the same session (like tabs) or split the current view into multiple panes, each running a separate shell. The keybindings differ significantly (`Ctrl+A c` for new window in screen, `Ctrl+B c` in tmux; `Ctrl+A S` for split in screen, `Ctrl+B %` or `"` for splits in tmux).

This is just a tiny glimpse. `screen` and `tmux` are powerful tools with many features for session management, window/pane control, copy-pasting, and configuration. We won't dive deeper here, but knowing they exist and understanding the core concepts of detaching and reattaching is crucial for managing long-running tasks and remote sessions effectively. Pick one (`tmux` is often recommended for new users due to its clearer configuration and features, but `screen` might be more readily available) and explore its tutorial or man page (`man screen`, `man tmux`) when you need this capability.

Chapter Summary

This chapter introduced a suite of powerful command-line utilities that significantly enhance your ability to process data and manage your workflow. You learned how `xargs` bridges the gap between standard input and command arguments, especially useful with `find` (using the robust `-print0/-0` combo). We explored `sed` for non-interactive stream editing, focusing on basic substitution (`s/.../.../`) and deletion (`d`). You met `awk`, the field-oriented pattern-processing language, perfect for extracting and manipulating columnar data. We covered `diff` for comparing file contents (especially the `-u` unified format), `wc` for counting lines/words/characters, `sort` for ordering data, and `uniq` for handling duplicate lines (usually after sorting). Finally, we briefly introduced the concept of terminal multiplexers (`screen`, `tmux`) for managing persistent sessions and multiple terminals within one window, crucial for remote work and long-running tasks.

These tools, often combined in pipelines, form the backbone of advanced command-line data manipulation and scripting. As you conclude the main instructional chapters of this book, you're equipped with a formidable set of skills. The final chapter will offer tips for improving your command-line efficiency, showcase some common workflows, provide troubleshooting advice, and point you toward further learning resources to continue your Linux mastery journey.

Chapter 17: Beyond the Basics

You've reached the final chapter of our command-line journey together! Take a moment to appreciate how far you've come. From tentatively typing your first commands like `date` and `pwd` (Chapter 1) to navigating the filesystem (Chapter 2), managing files (Chapter 3), viewing content (Chapter 4), getting help (Chapter 5), editing text (Chapter 6), understanding users and permissions (Chapter 7), controlling processes (Chapter 8), redirecting streams and building pipelines (Chapter 9), finding files and text (Chapter 10), customizing your shell environment (Chapter 11), archiving and compressing data (Chapter 12), managing software packages (Chapter 13), performing basic network tasks (Chapter 14), writing your first scripts (Chapter 15), and wielding power tools like `sed`, `awk`, and `xargs` (Chapter 16) – you've built a truly impressive foundation. The command line is no longer a mysterious black box; it's a powerful, flexible environment you can shape and control. This final chapter isn't about learning many *new* commands, but rather about consolidating your knowledge, picking up tips for greater efficiency, seeing how concepts combine in practical workflows, knowing how to troubleshoot common issues, and understanding where to explore next on your Linux adventure.

Tips for Command Line Efficiency

Working effectively on the command line isn't just about knowing the commands; it's also about using the shell's features to minimize effort and maximize speed. You've encountered many of these already, but let's reinforce them:

- **Master Tab Completion:** We introduced this back in Chapter 2, but it bears repeating. Use the `Tab` key relentlessly! It completes commands, filenames, directory paths, and even options for some commands. Pressing `Tab` twice often lists possible completions. This is your single biggest time-saver and typo-reducer.

- **Exploit Command History**: Don't retype long commands.
  - Use `Ctrl+R` to search backward incrementally through your history (as covered in Chapter 11). Type a few unique characters from the command you want, press `Ctrl+R` again if needed to find older matches, and hit `Enter` to execute or `Right Arrow` to edit.
  - Use `!!` to re-run the very last command (perfect for adding `sudo`).
  - Use `!string` to re-run the last command starting with `string` (use with slight caution).
  - Use `!n` to re-run command number n from the `history` list.
- **Create Useful Aliases**: Identify commands you type frequently with the same set of options. Turn them into short aliases in your `~/.bashrc` file (Chapter 11). Good candidates include:
  - `alias ll='ls -alh'`
  - `alias update='sudo apt update && sudo apt upgrade -y'` (or `sudo dnf upgrade -y`)
  - `alias pg='ps aux | grep'` (to quickly search processes)
  - `alias hg='history | grep'` (to quickly search history)
  - `alias ..='cd ..'`
  - `alias ...='cd ../..'`
- **Learn Basic Shell Functions (Advanced Aliases)**: For slightly more complex shortcuts that might involve arguments or simple logic, Bash **functions** offer more power than aliases. They are also defined in your `~/.bashrc`.
  - **Example**: A function to create a directory and then immediately change into it.

```
# Add this to ~/.bashrc
mkcd() {
   mkdir -p "$1" && cd "$1"
}
```

    After `source ~/.bashrc`, you can type `mkcd my_new_project` to create the directory and enter it in one step. `$1` represents the first argument passed to the function. This is essentially a very simple script defined directly within your shell's environment.
- **Use Keyboard Shortcuts**: Beyond `Ctrl+R`, `Ctrl+C`, and `Ctrl+Z`, learn other Bash readline shortcuts (many are Emacs-like by default):
  - `Ctrl+A`: Move cursor to the beginning of the line.
  - `Ctrl+E`: Move cursor to the end of the line.
  - `Ctrl+U`: Cut text from the cursor to the beginning of the line.

- Ctrl+K: Cut text from the cursor to the end of the line.
- Ctrl+W: Cut the word before the cursor.
- Ctrl+L: Clear the screen (like the clear command).
- Alt+B: Move cursor back one word.
- Alt+F: Move cursor forward one word.
- **Think in Pipelines:** As emphasized in Chapter 9, try to break down tasks into sequences of simpler commands connected by pipes (|). This is often more efficient and flexible than using complex command options or temporary files.

Common Workflows and Examples

Let's see how we can combine commands you've learned to accomplish practical tasks.

Log File Analysis

Imagine you want to find the most frequent IP addresses attempting to access a web server, based on an access log file (e.g., /var/log/nginx/access.log). Log lines might look something like:

```
1.2.3.4 - - [25/Jul/2024:16:30:01 +0100] "GET /page HTTP/1.1" 200 ...
```

We can use a pipeline:

1. cat /var/log/nginx/access.log: Get the file content (or use grep first if needed).
2. awk '{print $1}': Extract the first field (the IP address). awk splits lines by spaces by default.
3. sort: Sort the IP addresses alphabetically.
4. uniq -c: Count consecutive identical lines (which are now all identical IPs because of sort).
5. sort -nr: Sort the results numerically (-n) and in reverse order (-r) to get the highest counts first.
6. head -n 10: Show only the top 10 most frequent IPs.

The full pipeline (might need sudo to read the log):

```
sudo cat /var/log/nginx/access.log | awk '{print $1}' | \
  sort | uniq -c | sort -nr | head -n 10

  5432 192.168.10.50
```

```
1234 10.0.5.12
 987 8.8.8.8
 ... (top 10 IPs and their counts) ...
```

This concise pipeline performs a useful analysis by chaining together specialized tools.

System Monitoring Snippets

Need to keep an eye on a specific process or disk usage?

- **Watch a specific process's resource usage:** Combine ps aux (Chapter 8), grep (Chapter 10), and the watch command (which runs a command repeatedly, displaying its output).

  ```
  # Update every 2 seconds (default), showing firefox process info
  watch 'ps aux | grep firefox | grep -v grep'
  ```

  (grep -v grep *is often used to exclude the* grep *command itself from the results. Press* Ctrl+C *to exit* watch.)

- **Monitor free disk space:**

  ```
  watch df -h
  ```

  (df -h *shows disk free space in human-readable format.*)

Batch File Operations

Let's rename all .jpeg files in the current directory to .jpg safely, handling spaces or weird characters in filenames. We use the find/xargs pattern from Chapter 16 and a small loop within the xargs command using sh -c.

```
# Create test files
touch image1.jpeg "photo two.jpeg" "file three.JPEG"

# Find .jpeg files (case-insensitive), pass null-separated to xargs
find . -maxdepth 1 -iname "*.jpeg" -type f -print0 | \
  xargs -0 -I {} sh -c 'mv -v "{}" "$(basename "{}" .jpeg).jpg"'

# Or handle different cases like .JPEG
find . -maxdepth 1 \( -iname "*.jpeg" -o -iname "*.JPEG" \) -type f -print0 | \
  xargs -0 -I {} sh -c '
```

```
oldname="{}"
# Get base name without extension (case-insensitive removal)
base=$(basename "$oldname" .jpeg 2>/dev/null || basename "$oldname" .JPEG)
# Construct new name
newname="$base.jpg"
# Only rename if new name is different (prevents errors if already .jpg)
if [ "$oldname" != "$newname" ]; then
    mv -v "$oldname" "$newname"
fi
'
```

(This is more advanced, using -I *{} to process one file at a time within a mini-script passed to* sh -c, basename *to manipulate the filename, and command substitution. It demonstrates combining tools for robust batch operations.)*

These examples show how individual commands become building blocks for more sophisticated solutions.

Troubleshooting Common Issues

As you work more with the command line, you'll inevitably encounter errors. Here are some common ones and how to approach them:

- command not found:

  - **Typo:** Did you spell the command name correctly? Remember Linux is case-sensitive (Ls is not ls).
  - **Not Installed:** Is the program actually installed? Use your package manager (apt search <cmd> or dnf search <cmd>, Chapter 13) to check and install if necessary.
  - **Not in PATH:** Is the command located in a directory listed in your $PATH environment variable (Chapter 11)? If it's a custom script or program in the current directory, you need to run it with ./command. If it's installed elsewhere, you might need to add its directory to your PATH (by editing ~/.bash_profile or ~/.bashrc). Use which command or type command (Chapter 5) to see if the shell can locate it.

- Permission denied:

  - **File Permissions:** Do you have the necessary permissions (read, write, or execute) on the file or directory you're trying to access? Use ls -l (Chapter 7) to check ownership and permissions. You might need chmod to change permissions (if you own the file) or sudo if the operation requires root privileges. Remember you need execute (x) permission on a directory to `cd` into it or access files within it.

- **Execute Permission:** If trying to run a script, did you make it executable with `chmod +x scriptname` (Chapter 15)?
- **Filesystem Mount Options:** Sometimes, filesystems (especially removable drives) might be mounted with options like `noexec` that prevent running programs from them. (Check `mount` command output).

- `No such file or directory`:

  - **Typo:** Did you spell the filename or path correctly? Case sensitivity matters!
  - **Wrong Directory:** Are you in the correct directory (`pwd`)? Does the file actually exist where you think it does (`ls path/to/file`)?
  - **Relative vs. Absolute Path:** Are you using the correct type of path (Chapter 2)? Does your relative path make sense from your current location?

- **Problems with Spaces or Special Characters in Filenames:**

  - **Quoting:** Always enclose filenames containing spaces or special characters (like `*`, `?`, `&`, `$`) in double quotes (`"filename with spaces"`).
  - find/xargs: Use the `find ... -print0 | xargs -0 ...` pattern for safe processing (Chapter 16).
  - **Tab Completion:** Let tab completion handle the quoting and escaping for you whenever possible!

- **"Too many arguments" or unexpected command behavior:** Often caused by unquoted variables or command substitutions that expand to multiple words when you expected only one. Always quote your variables (`"$variable"`) and command substitutions (`"$(command)"`) unless you specifically need word splitting.

When faced with an error, **read the error message carefully**. It often contains valuable clues. Break down complex commands into smaller parts to isolate where the error is occurring. Use `echo` within scripts to print variable values and trace execution flow.

The Linux Community and Finding More Help

You are never alone on your Linux journey! One of the greatest strengths of Linux and open-source software is the vast, helpful community surrounding it. When you get stuck, remember the resources available:

1. **Built-in Help (Your First Stop!):**
   - `man command` (Chapter 5): The official manual pages. Comprehensive but sometimes dense.
   - `info command` (Chapter 5): Hypertext documentation, often detailed for GNU tools.
   - `command --help` (Chapter 5): Quick usage summary and options list for many commands.
   - `help` (Bash built-in): Get help on shell built-in commands like `cd`, `type`, `read`.
2. **Online Resources:**
   - **Search Engines:** Your favorite search engine is often the fastest way to find solutions to specific error messages or "how-to" guides. Prefix searches with "linux" or your distribution name (e.g., "ubuntu add user to group").
   - **Distribution Documentation:** Ubuntu, Fedora, Debian, Arch Linux, etc., all have excellent official documentation, wikis, and tutorials on their websites.
   - **Q&A Sites:** Stack Overflow, Ask Ubuntu, Unix & Linux Stack Exchange are invaluable. Search for existing answers before asking a new question. Learn how to ask well-defined questions with relevant details (error messages, commands used, expected vs. actual output).
   - **Forums and Mailing Lists:** Many distributions and specific projects have active user forums or mailing lists.
   - **IRC/Matrix/Discord:** Real-time chat channels can be helpful but often require patience and clear communication.

Be persistent, learn how to search effectively, and don't be afraid to consult the documentation or ask the community (after doing your own research first!).

Where to Go Next

This book has aimed to give you a solid mastery of the Linux command line fundamentals. But there's always more to learn! Where you go next depends on your interests:

- **Advanced Shell Scripting:** Dive deeper into Bash scripting features like functions, arrays, traps (handling signals), regular expressions, and interaction with tools like `sed` and `awk`. Look for dedicated scripting tutorials or books.
- **System Administration:** If you want to manage Linux servers, explore topics like user/group management in depth, disk partitioning and filesystems (`fdisk`, `mkfs`, `/etc/fstab`), network configuration (`ip`, `nmcli`, firewall tools like `ufw` or `firewalld`), service management (`systemctl`), process monitoring in depth, logging (`journalctl`), and security hardening.
- **Specific Tools:** Master tools relevant to your work:
    - `git`: Version control system (essential for developers and often useful for administrators managing configurations).
    - `docker/podman`: Containerization technologies for packaging and deploying applications.
    - `ansible/puppet/chef`: Configuration management and automation tools.
    - Text Editors: Become truly proficient in `vim` or explore other powerful editors like Emacs.
- **Programming on Linux:** Learn languages like Python, C, C++, Go, Rust, or others. The Linux command line is an excellent environment for software development, providing powerful compilers, debuggers, and build tools.
- **Networking In-Depth:** Explore tools like `tcpdump` and Wireshark for packet analysis, understand network protocols (TCP/IP, UDP, HTTP, DNS) more deeply, and learn about network routing and firewalls.
- **Try Different Distributions/Shells:** Experimenting with other Linux distributions (like Arch Linux for more manual configuration or Fedora for cutting-edge software) or different shells (like `zsh` with frameworks like Oh My Zsh, or `fish` for user-friendliness) can broaden your perspective.

The key is to keep practicing, experimenting in safe environments (like virtual machines), and building things. Find small problems you can solve or tasks you can automate using the command line.

Keep Exploring!

The Linux command line is a gateway to immense computing power and flexibility. It might have seemed daunting at first, but by progressing through these chapters, you've acquired the skills to confidently interact with, manage, and automate Linux systems. The learning never truly stops; there's always a new command, a more elegant technique, or a deeper concept to explore. Embrace the journey, stay curious, leverage the community, and enjoy the power you now wield at your fingertips. Happy typing!

Chapter Summary

This concluding chapter focused on consolidating your command-line mastery and guiding your next steps. We reviewed essential **efficiency techniques**, emphasizing tab completion, history usage, aliases, and the potential of shell functions. We illustrated how to combine commands into practical **workflows** for tasks like log analysis, system monitoring, and batch file operations. Key **troubleshooting** strategies were discussed for common errors like `command not found` and `Permission denied`, stressing the importance of reading error messages and checking permissions, paths, and spelling. We reinforced the value of leveraging both built-in help (`man`, `info`, `--help`) and the extensive **online Linux community** for support. Finally, we suggested several avenues for **further learning**, including advanced scripting, system administration, specific power tools, programming, networking, and exploring different distributions or shells. The command line is a vast and rewarding environment; this book has given you the map and compass – now go explore!

www.ingramcontent.com/pod-product-compliance
Lightning Source LLC
LaVergne TN
LVHW081341050326
832903LV00024B/1250